PORTABELLA
MUSHROOM
PARTY

TROY BROWN

Photo Credits

I want to thank my exclusive photographer who helped me in all the photo shoots in both the photos and the creative layout for each shoot.

Paul Titangos at Santa Cruz, California.
Titangos Photography Studio
216-A Fern Street, Santa Cruz, CA 95060
831-423-8786 www.titangos.com

Table of Contents

Recipes

Acknowledgments

I want to thank my mother, Jo Neatha Bass, for teaching me the joys of cooking and for giving me positive encouragement during this project.

My sister, JoMerril Brown.

I am grateful to my dear wife, Margot Brown, for spending hours upon hours helping me type the manuscript.

My wonderful neighbors for tasting and evaluating all of the dishes and recipes for me.

Ultimately,

I am appreciative to all my friends from all walks of life who have consistently given me positive feedback telling me "You can do it!"

Especially Ken Harlan.

Finally,

I want to sincerely thank my friend, employer and fishing buddy, Ken Harlan (known as Kenny) proprietor of Lucia Lodge in Big Sur, California.

IN MEMORY OF ...
BOB RUSSIN
DR. SANDI TATMAN

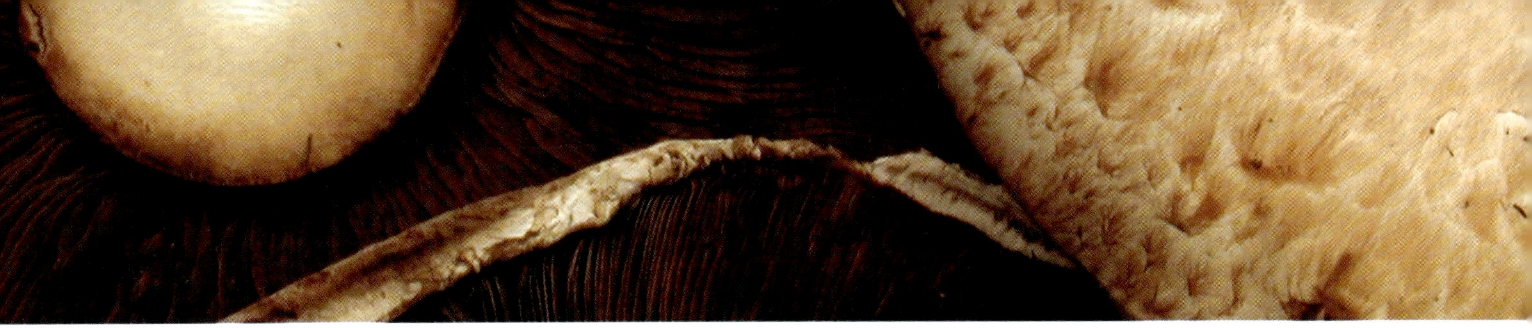

It all began one evening...

when my wife and I went out for an Italian dinner with friends. The portabella appetizer was OK, but my first thought was, "This could be prepared better".

This began much experimentation, preparation and enthusiastic conversation with a variety of people over time. My message was the same.

"I have found a new way to prepare portabellas...They are DELICIOUS!"

Over time, as I got better they tasted even more exquisite than imaginable and the taste buds of my friends expanded to include the magic of portabellas.

What I found out was that overall, people were uninformed about portabellas. I would stand in line at the grocery store with several packages of portabellas and unbelievably both men and women would leave their place in line to cross over to me asking a variety of questions.

THEIR QUESTIONS INCLUDED THE FOLLOWING...

"How do you cook those?"

"I've tasted them, but I don't know how to cook them."

"I only know one way to cook those."

"I have only had them in a restaurant and they were not very good."

"I've never tasted those."

"What kind of spice do you use on them?"

"Those are huge, are those mushrooms?"

(It became a running joke between me and my wife as to how many people approached me at the grocery store today.) As time passed, and as the people varied from neighbors, to visiting friends from back east, to 49er tailgating friends, from people who owned restaurants and businesses, one thing was revealed to me over and over...They liked the way I cooked portabellas and they couldn't believe it was a mushroom! The expressions on their faces when they tasted it, said it all—amazement!

That's when I decided to create a cookbook so others could experience the joy and accomplishment of cooking something new—without much difficulty.

At first, I approached a friend to help me with the cookbook. Unfortunately, after a while, he was unable to continue due to a variety of life changes. The good thing, however, was that during the first few months of organizing the cookbook, we developed a friendly competition in the kitchen about who could come up with the best-tasting, most unique way of cooking portabella mushrooms. Let me tell you—those were some phenomenal cookouts! We would sit to a feast of four or five portabella dishes, from appetizers to salad to main course! It was fun and delicious! During that time I began to believe that my dream was closer to materializing. Eventually, after more cookouts than you can count, I continued cooking, organizing and writing the recipes I had been accumulating for more than half a year.

The recipes in this book borrow from a variety of

ETHNIC CATEGORIES:

Italian, Asian, Mexican, Mediterranean

AS WELL AS TYPES OF CLASSIFICATIONS:

Appetizers, Soups and Entrees

Many of the recipes have originated from my own experimental nature and others have stemmed from themes of other cooking styles. My hope is you will enjoy them all.

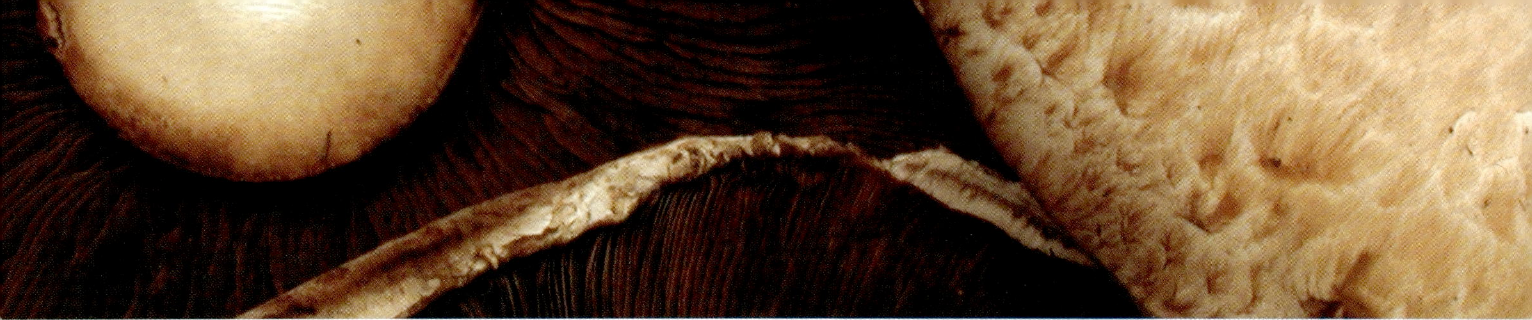

General Information About Portabellas

ORIGINS

In the past, mushrooms have symbolized the magical, the mysterious and even the supernatural aspect of life. This aura of association remains true for many. In our literature and folklore, mushrooms are a constant reminder of that which is unexplainably ancient and rooted in the earth as powerful.

HOW DO YOU SPELL IT?
HOW DO YOU SAY IT?

According to Wikipedia (2012),...

"Among English speakers, *Agaricus bisporus* is known by many names. A young specimen with a closed cap and either pale white or light brown flesh is known as **button mushroom** or **white mushroom.** In strains with darker flesh, the immature mushroom is variously marketed as a **crimini mushroom, baby portobello, baby bella, mini bella, portabellini, Roman mushroom, Italian mushroom,** or **brown mushroom.** At this stage of maturation, the cap may also begin to open slightly. In maturity, it is called a **portobello.** The French name is *champignon de Paris* ("Paris mushroom")."

Both spellings of *portabella* (or *portobella*) and *portobello* are used, although the former is preferred in some circles. In this book, I consistently refer to this mushroom as "portabella".

PORTABELLAS ARE GIANT CRIMINI MUSHROOMS

They are much larger than the range of other species and look huge to the novice mushroom consumer. The cap is large and the stem is tough (should be cut off and used for stock or discarded). Their flavor is meaty and their substance is filling. Portabellas take well to grilling on the BBQ, roasting in the oven or sautéing in a skillet. When grilling or roasting, place them gill (stem) side down at first, to be rotated later.

STORING OF MUSHROOMS

Mushrooms in plastic bags sweat in their own heat, eventually becoming slippery and unappetizing. Store mushrooms unwashed inside a brown paper bag. When purchasing mushrooms in cellophane-wrapped containers, be sure to transfer to a paper bag and place in the vegetable bin of the refrigerator as soon as possible.

Store between 34°F and 38°F.

Do not store near pungent items in your refrigerator.

Do not store with garlic, onions or bananas.

DO NOT FREEZE uncooked portabellas because they retain excess water when frozen.

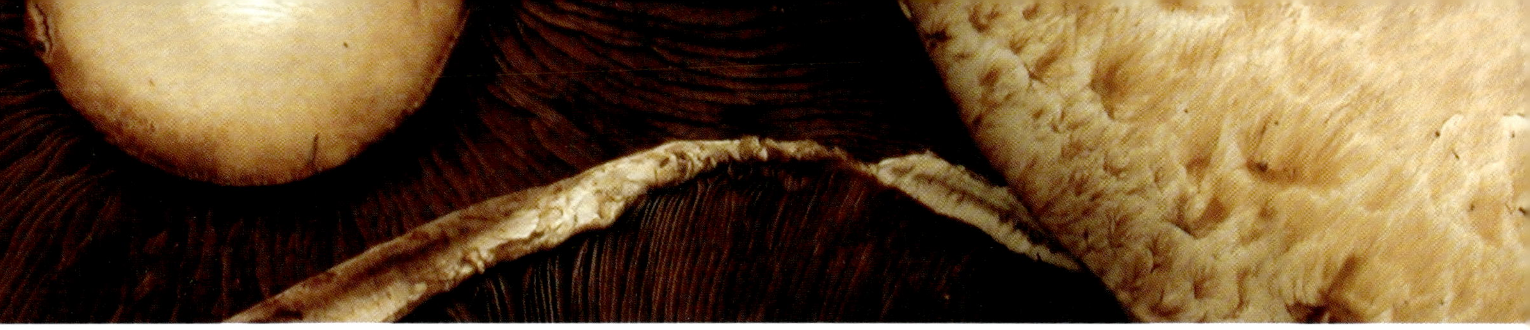

WASHING AND PREPARATION OF MUSHROOMS

Mushrooms should not be washed, but rather wiped with a damp cloth or piece of paper towel to retain their flavor. Never immerse mushrooms in a bowl of water to clean. Mushrooms are 90% water; you do not want to increase their moisture content. Waterlogged mushrooms are more difficult to cook properly. The excess water alters the texture. Handle with care; portabellas bruise easily.

Note: Some people prefer to remove the gills from the portabellas. If the gills are not removed, some of the recipes (such as cream sauced recipes) may become darker in color. If you choose to, you can simply scrape off the gills with a small paring knife or small spoon to avoid any darkness in some of the soups, cream sauces, etc.

COOKING MUSHROOMS

You will notice that mushrooms shrink noticeably during cooking. They absorb fat as they cook, so it is best to use butter or preferably a good olive oil for frying. Sauté mushrooms over a moderately high heat. As they shrink, the water should evaporate so that they do not simmer in their own watery juices. It is important to not overpack the sautéing pan or skillet when frying mushrooms. Too many jumbled mushrooms in one pan will slow down the cooking process and will only create a pyramid effect that results in a watery mess.

NUTRITIONAL INFORMATION

	% Daily Value		% Daily Value
Serving Size 4 Slices (85g)	100%	Dietary Fiber 3g	12%
Calories 20	0%	Sugars 1g	0%
Calories From Fat None	0%	Vitamin A	0%
Total Fat None	0%	Vitamin C	0%
Saturated Fat None	0%	Calcium	4%
Cholesterol None	0%	Iron	2%
Sodium 10mg	0%	Total Carbohydrate 4g	1%
		Protein 3g	0%

*Percent Daily Values are based on a 2,000 calorie diet.

Getting Ready In the Kitchen

What You Will Need

As you read the recipes you will see there are primarily three methods of cooking:

Grilling on the BBQ,
Sautéing in a frying pan and
Broiling in the oven.

You will need a frying pan, a sauté pan and a pizza or cookie sheet for broiling in the oven. For those gas ranges that have their own separate broiling section, use the broiling rack provided. In addition, you can use a wooden, plastic or metal spatula. Or, a long/short pair of tongs and a sharp knife will be your best utensils.

In this book, olive oil is used more often than corn oil or butter. There is an enormous range of taste and flavors in olive oil. Extra virgin olive oil is the top grade of olive oil. It is a virgin or unprocessed oil, which has the lowest acidity level.

When Recipes Call for Heating Olive Oil in a Large Skillet

Many of the recipes call for heating olive oil in a skillet. It takes approximately ⅛ cup of olive oil to cover the bottom of a large skillet.

When heating the skillet over medium-high heat, it takes approximately 4 minutes for the skillet to become hot. Of course, it depends on the type of skillet you use. If it is a cast iron skillet, it will usually take longer to heat up than a stainless steel skillet or a non-stick skillet. You must use your judgement and your own knowledge of your cooking utensils as to the exact length of time needed before adding the mushrooms.

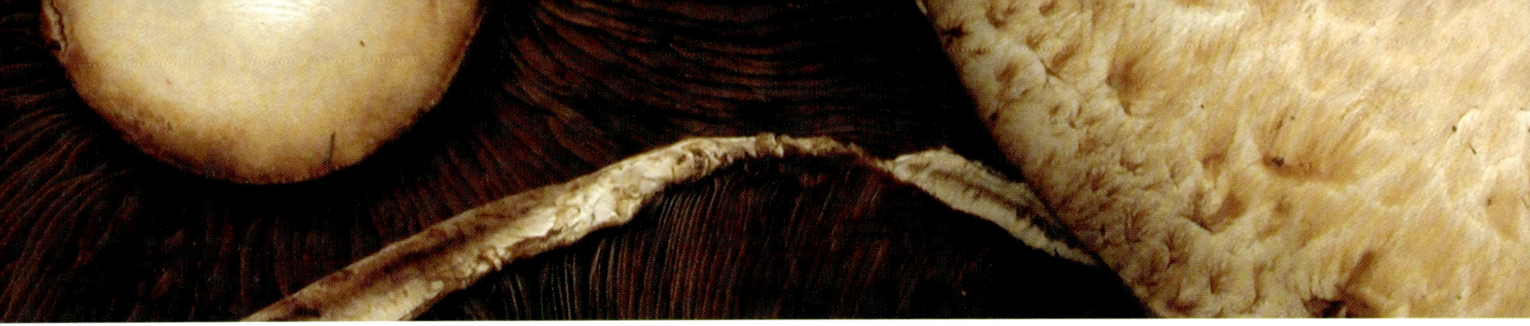

Spices

What is life without spice? In this book, the most frequently used spice among many, is the Cajun spice, which I make from scratch with organic spices that I purchase by the pound. There are many excellent premixed Cajun spices in your local grocery store, including some without salt. I have a strong bias toward Cajun spice as it lends itself to portabellas nicely. Also, when you grill the Cajun portabellas the Cajun spice drips down on the coals, which makes the mushrooms mild in flavor and leaves you with a pleasant aftertaste of spice without the fire. If you choose to sauté the Cajun portabella you must use less spice as the spice remains in the pan with the portabellas.

Every individual is different and you should always keep that in mind as you prepare your own dish. If you do not prefer as many spices, or hot ones, then find mild spices, or use salt and pepper to your liking. It does not matter. That is the beauty of creativity and personal choice. Use the recipes in this book as a guideline in your determination of what it is you like! The portabellas are the magic and the accoutrements only accent the essence. So choose your own accents.

Seasoning Recipes

Troy's Handmade Cajun Spice Recipe

1 tsp. onion powder
1 tsp. cayenne pepper
1 tsp. black pepper
1½ tbsp. paprika
(You may add more for redness)
½ tsp. oregano
¼ tsp. salt

1 tsp. garlic powder
1 tsp. white pepper
½ tsp. thyme
½ tsp. basil
¼ tsp. chili powder

There are many excellent premade commercial Mexican spices but if you want to create your own, try this:

Mexican Seasoning

½ tsp. paprika
½ tsp. onion powder
½ tsp. chili powder
½ tsp. sugar
¼ tsp. oregano

¼ tsp. chili peppers
¼ tsp. garlic powder
¼ tsp. cayenne pepper
¼ tsp. black pepper

SAUCE AND DRESSING RECIPES

A Variation on Premixed Italian Dressing for Marinade

¼ cup vinegar (balsamic)
1 package Good Seasons spices
1 tsp. mustard (dry or wet)
1 tsp. minced garlic

½ cup olive oil (extra virgin)
1 tsp. ketchup
2 tsp. sugar

Troy's Homemade Barbecue Sauce

2 cups ketchup
⅛ cup molasses
½ tsp. black pepper
¼ cup vinegar (cider, white, wine, rice)

½ cup mustard
¼ cup Worcestershire sauce

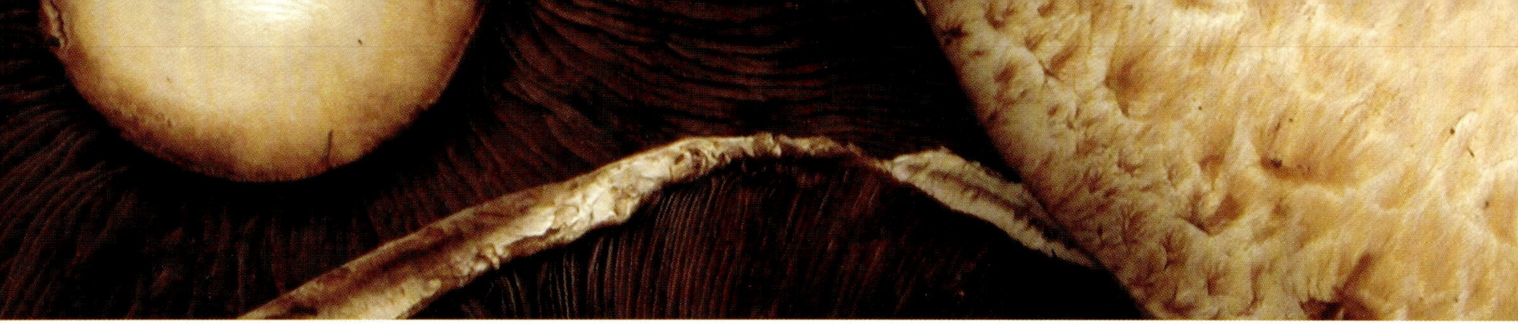

CREATIVITY

Remember, I am a fan of Cajun spice. If you have a favorite spice you love to use more than others, I encourage you to use that particular spice when cooking portabellas for several reasons. First, you may not like the spicy flavor that Cajun brings. Second, you are comfortable with your favorite spice and therefore you are familiar with using it and should continue to use it to your liking. Third, after you master cooking portabellas with your own spice, then you may be more inclined to try experimenting with other spices including Cajun spice.

The most important focus of this book is to get people to start cooking with portabellas!!!! That is the key. The magic of cooking with portabellas can be a new beginning for you in the kitchen and out on the grill.

CONGRATULATIONS!

You are opening up to a new world of cooking in your life! Have fun and enjoy!

TROY BROWN

HOW TO READ THE RECIPES IN THIS BOOK

Many of the recipe titles do not contain the word "portabella." After much deliberation, it was decided that the reader would tire of reading "portabella" in each title. So, please remember and assume that each and every recipe regardless of its title has portabella mushrooms in it! Whenever the word "mushroom" is used, it means portabella mushrooms unless another variety is specified.

Titles Without Flair

As you read this book it is also apparent that I chose not to create flashy stylish, zippy titles, such as Zesty Pizza with Portabellas or Cajun Ravioli That Knocks Your Socks Off! Portabellas speak for themselves. They are such a special mushroom/vegetable. They can be chameleons if you wish them to be by changing your choice of spices, subtly adding a unique flair to the overall flavor of the dish. However, they are themselves unique, meaty, large and distinctive in taste. As a result, they can't help but be noticed as the center of attention that they justly deserve. So, a zippy title they do not need. Portabellas have their own voice and they stand at attention on their own, with pride and distinction. I hope you agree.

APPETIZERS
SOUPS & SUCH

Baked Whole Portabellas

Ingredients:

4	whole portabella mushrooms, remove stems
½	cup bread crumbs
¼	cup parmesan cheese
1	medium tomato, chopped
	olive oil

1. Brush each side of whole portabella with olive oil until completely coated. Bake at 375°F for 30 minutes in preheated oven with stem side down.
2. In a separate bowl, combine bread crumbs with cheese.
3. Remove mushrooms from oven and turn cap side down. Fill with bread crumbs/cheese mixture. Top with chopped tomatoes. Return mushrooms to oven for 5 minutes. Remove, serve immediately.

SERVES 4.

APPETIZERS, SOUPS & SUCH

Breaded and Pan or Creole Fried

Ingredients:

1	cup bread crumbs
2	eggs well beaten
4	portabella mushrooms, sliced
⅛	cup olive oil
1–2	tsp. Creole seasoning (optional)
¼	cup milk (optional)
	salt and pepper to taste

1. Pour bread crumbs* into a shallow bowl.
2. Beat eggs in a separate shallow dish (with a small amount of milk, approximately ¼ cup, if desired). Dredge portabellas through egg dish and then bread crumb mixture.
3. In a large skillet, at medium-high heat, cover bottom of pan with olive oil to prepare for cooking.
4. Place mushrooms in hot skillet and fry until golden brown on all sides (turn every 2 minutes). Remove to paper towel when done. Serve immediately. Add salt and pepper to taste.

SERVES 4–6.

*Note: To make Creole-fried mushrooms, mix 1–2 tsp. Creole seasoning with bread crumbs before dredging mushrooms.

Stuffed Artichokes

Ingredients:

4	medium artichokes
	(see below for preparation)
2	portabella mushrooms, diced
⅛	cup olive oil
1	cup bread crumbs
2	cloves minced garlic
½	cup mozzarella cheese, grated
2–3	tbsp. olive oil
½	cup crumbled feta cheese
8	tsp. dry white wine
	lemon juice as needed

1. Remove stems from artichokes. Trim away exterior tough leaves. Cut and remove top third. Remove soft interior leaves and hairy inner part. Wash and rinse thoroughly in a bowl of water. To maintain color add a few drops of lemon juice.
2. Cover bottom of large skillet with olive oil. Add mushrooms and cook over medium high heat for 15 minutes until moisture is reduced. Remove.
3. Mix together bread crumbs, mushrooms, garlic, mozzarella cheese, feta cheese and 2 tablespoons of olive oil in a bowl.
4. Drain artichokes and pat dry. Fill cavity with cheese/mushroom mixture. Top with a few extra tablespoons of the bread crumb mixture (step 3).
5. Sprinkle white wine (2 tsp.) on each artichoke. Place in baking pan and add enough water to cover bottom half of chokes. Bake in preheated oven at 350ºF for 35 minutes or until done. Serve immediately.

SERVES 4.

Portabella Brie Cheese Sandwich

Ingredients:

4	portabella mushrooms, sliced
6–8	tbsp. olive oil
1	head lettuce (butter, romaine, iceberg), washed, torn leaves
1	medium tomato, sliced
1	medium yellow onion, sliced
6	soft French rolls, split
1	8-oz. block Brie cheese, at room temperature.
	Cajun seasoning

1. Place sliced portabella mushrooms in large bowl. Add olive oil and Cajun seasoning. Toss until each slice is well coated.
2. Continue to toss every 15 minutes for 30–45 minutes prior to grilling. If mushrooms become dry add more olive oil to coat each mushroom. Do not saturate with oil, only lightly coat with the olive oil. Continue to add Cajun spice every time you coat with oil.
3. Grill preparation: When coals on grill are gray and ready, place each mushroom slice on grill. Cook for 5 minutes; turn mushrooms and continue to cook for 5 minutes more. Grill will be hot; you must watch mushrooms as the olive oil will make the grill flame. Cover grill with lid until flame subsides (if needed).
4. Split French rolls and heat on grill. Remove rolls from grill and spread Brie cheese evenly over bread. Place grilled mushrooms on roll; add lettuce, tomato and onions. Serve immediately.

SERVES 6.

APPETIZERS, SOUPS & SUCH

Chili Portabella Tart with Potato

Ingredients for Tart:

1⅓	cups flour
¼	tsp. salt
6–8	tbsp. unsalted butter
1	red or green chili pepper, seeded, finely chopped
¼	cup parmesan cheese, grated
	cold water as needed

Ingredients for Filling

2	portabella mushrooms, diced
⅛	cup olive oil
4	cloves of minced garlic
4	medium potatoes (washed, peeled)
1¼	cups whipping cream, lightly whipped
1	tsp. salt
1	tsp. coarse ground black pepper

1. Start by making pastry tart. First, sift flour and salt in bowl. Cut butter into mixture until flour is formed into crumbs. Add chopped chili pepper (no seeds) and parmesan cheese. Add cold water one tablespoon at a time. Stir dough with a large wooden spoon until it is no longer crumbly. It should stick together to form a firm large ball.

2. Add a light sprinkle of flour to working surface (wood or marble) before rolling out the dough. Roll out dough onto working surface. To transfer rolled dough to a tart pan (or quiche dish), begin at the edge and roll dough towards you on the rolling pin, lift rolling pin and dough to tart pan (or quiche dish), and unroll dough by rolling pin away from you into tart pan. The dough should smoothly unfold onto the dish. Flute edges of dough on pan. Prick bottom of crust with a fork and chill for 30 minutes. After 30 minutes remove pan from refrigerator and preheat oven to 400ºF. Cover bottom of tart pan with foil. Prebake for 10–15 minutes so that dough will be partially done. Remove from oven. Remove foil from pan.

3. In large skillet add olive oil (⅛ cup). At medium-high heat cook mushrooms for 10 minutes until moisture is reduced. Add minced garlic and cook 5 minutes more.

4. Wash and skin potatoes. In a large soup pot boil enough water to cover potatoes. Cook approximately 30 minutes until done. Remove and slice thinly.

5. Place whipping cream in a bowl, add salt and pepper to taste and whip lightly. Whip cream until it folds and retains consistency. Do not whip until stiff peaks form. The purpose is to partially whip the cream so that it is not fluid like milk, but not too stiffly whipped, either.

6. Increase oven temperature to 450ºF. Spread mushrooms to cover bottom of prebaked tart shell. Layer sliced potatoes over mushrooms, then pour cream over the top. Bake at high heat (450°F) for 8–10 minutes, until top is golden brown. Serve immediately.

SERVES 4–6.

APPETIZERS, SOUPS & SUCH

Portabella Dumplings

Ingredients:

Dough:
(or use pot sticker squares from most grocery stores)

2	cups water
4	cups white flour
½	tsp. salt
2	tbsp. oil

1. In a pot bring the water to boil. In a separate large bowl, mix flour and salt. Add boiling water and oil in small amounts while continuously stirring. Continue to stir until dough separates from bowl and becomes sticky. Knead the dough on a floured work surface until it becomes smooth and elastic. Form the dough into a ball, replace in the bowl and place a damp cloth over the dough. Let it sit for 45 minutes to 1 hour.
2. Take dough and form into two parts. On a floured work surface, roll one part into a long thin sausage log roll. Cut into ½-inch slices. Take each slice and flatten in the palm of your hand, then use roller to flatten into a circular wrapper.
3. Follow steps below for filling. Repeat steps for second part of dough.

Filling for Dumplings:

2	portabella mushrooms, diced
1	medium Chinese cabbage (or regular), chopped
2	tbsp. finely chopped fresh ginger
1–2	tbsp. soy sauce
6–8	long green onions, chopped
1	egg, beaten
3	tbsp. sesame oil
¼	cup sesame oil – to cook dumplings in skillet
⅛	cup olive oil, to sauté mushrooms

1. In a large skillet, add ⅛ cup olive oil, and sauté diced mushrooms for 8 minutes until done. Remove mushrooms from skillet and place in large bowl. In same bowl combine the following: cabbage, ginger, soy sauce, onions, egg and 3 tbsp. sesame oil. Mix until evenly coated.
2. Take each wrapper dough and fill with 1–2 tbsp. of filling mixture (step 1). Fold wrapper in half and begin pressing the edges at one end and continue to the opposite side. Be careful not to fill too much or filling will leak out. The edge should be sealed. If necessary use a tsp. of water on your finger to help seal the edges. Place dumpling sealed side down.
3. First pour ¼ cup oil in large skillet. Heat over high heat. Cook several dumplings at a time, being careful not to let them touch each other. Cook for 6–7 minutes, turning until golden brown. Remove to paper towel.
4. While continuing to cook dumplings, preheat oven to 150ºF and place cooked dumplings in baking dish covered with foil to keep warm until ready to serve. Use dipping sauce of your choice or soy sauce. When done, remove dumplings from oven and arrange with last batch of recently fried dumplings. Serve immediately.

SERVES 4.

APPETIZERS, SOUPS & SUCH

Teriyaki Burger

Ingredients:

4	whole portabella mushrooms, remove stems
2	cups teriyaki sauce
4	soft French bread rolls
	Garnish Options: tomato, lettuce, onions

1. Place portabella mushrooms in a large bowl. Add teriyaki sauce. Toss until each slice is well coated. Toss every 15 minutes for 45 minutes to 1 hour.
2. When coals on grill* are gray and ready, place mushrooms on grill and cook each side for 5 minutes. Remove immediately.
3. If preferred, place French rolls on grill to warm or brown. Serve one portabella per bun. Garnish as preferred. Serve immediately.

Serves 4.

*An indoor grill could be used as an alternative.

APPETIZERS, SOUPS & SUCH

Sweet Potatoes and Yams

Ingredients:

⅔	cup olive oil
3	portabella mushrooms, diced
1	large sweet potato, diced
1	large yam, diced
8	green onions, chopped
2	tbsp. coconut syrup

1. Cover bottom of two separate large skillets with olive oil (⅓ cup) at medium-high heat. Cook mushrooms in first skillet for 15 minutes. Simultaneously, in the other skillet cook sweet potato and yam until tender (approximately 15 minutes). Add chopped onions during the last 5 minutes of cooking.
2. Add mushrooms and coconut syrup to potato mixture, and serve on large platter.

SERVES 4–6.

Potato Pancake

Ingredients:

⅛	cup olive oil
3	portabella mushrooms, diced
1	large onion, sliced
1	clove minced garlic
2	medium carrots, peeled and grated
2	medium zucchini, trimmed and grated
4	medium potatoes, shredded
½	cup medium cheddar cheese, grated
	salt and pepper to taste

1. In large skillet, cover bottom of skillet with olive oil. Heat over medium-high heat. Place mushrooms in skillet and cook for 10 minutes until moisture is removed. Add onions and garlic and continue cooking for 5 minutes or more (until onions are transparent). When done remove immediately and pour into a large bowl.

2. Grate carrots, zucchini and potatoes. Mix together in a large bowl (step 1).

3. Take large skillet with ovenproof handle and cover bottom with olive oil and cook over medium-high heat. Pour cooked grated mixture from step 1 and step 2 into skillet. Stir and cook for approximately 5–7 minutes. Then flatten potato mixture in skillet with spatula but do not stir. Cook for another 6–10 minutes until pancake is browned on the underside and almost cooked completely through.

4. Remove skillet from stovetop and sprinkle grated cheese on top of pancake. Then place skillet under broiler for 5 minutes or until cheese is completely melted and pancake is golden brown on top. Remove from broiler. Cut into wedges and serve immediately as a hot dish. As a cold side dish, wrap each wedge in plastic wrap and refrigerate until needed.

SERVES 6–8.

Portabella Toast

Ingredients:

½	cube butter
4	portabella mushrooms, diced
6–8	green onions, chopped
1	clove garlic, minced
¼	cup heavy whipping cream
4	slices of bread toasted
	parsley, chopped
	salt and pepper to taste

1. Heat butter in sauté pan. Add chopped mushrooms and cook over medium-high heat for 8 minutes. Add chopped onions, garlic and salt and pepper. Continue cooking for another 4 minutes.
2. Reduce heat. Add cream to the mushroom mixture and simmer for another 15 minutes, stirring until mushrooms are coated with a creamy reduction.
3. Toast bread and place on a platter. When the mushroom mixture is thick and creamy, pour over toast. Sprinkle with chopped parsley. Serve immediately as an appetizer.

SERVES 4.

APPETIZERS, SOUPS & SUCH

Thanksgiving Stuffing

Ingredients:*

Make cornbread following cornmeal
box directions

2	cubes butter
1	medium yellow onion, diced
4–6	stalks celery, chopped
4–6	tsp. sage (or more to taste)
1	bag white seasoned stuffing mix (croutons)
⅛	cup olive oil
2–4	portabella mushrooms, diced
2	eggs, beaten
2	medium cans of chicken broth (or more if needed)

1. While baking cornbread according to instructions, take large skillet and begin melting one cube butter. At medium heat, add chopped onions, celery and sage. Stir until onions are transparent. Add croutons to skillet and stir until bread cubes are evenly coated with butter and spice.

2. Pour ⅛ cup olive oil in a separate large skillet. Add mushrooms and cook over medium heat for 10–15 minutes until moisture is reduced down.

3. When cornbread is done, remove from oven and scrape directly (while hot) into an extra large bowl. Add one cube butter to hot cornbread in bowl. Add crouton mixture from skillet (step 1). Add cooked portabellas from second skillet.

4. Add two eggs to mixture in bowl and stir. Add chicken broth and continue to stir until well moistened and evenly mixed.

5. Pour mixture from bowl into a large 9" × 12" greased glass baking dish. Press down evenly across the top. Cover and refrigerate until ready to bake.

6. Bake uncovered at 375ºF degrees for 35–40 minutes until golden brown. Serve immediately.

Sᴇʀᴠᴇs 16.

*This recipe can be made ahead of time in the morning and baked 45 minutes before turkey is ready.

APPETIZERS, SOUPS & SUCH

Potato and Onion Fritter

Ingredients:

3–4	medium potatoes, peeled, quartered
2	minced garlic cloves
6	green onions, chopped
2–3	portabella mushrooms, diced
1	egg yolk
2½	cups bread crumbs
¼	cup olive oil (use in two parts)
2	eggs, well beaten
	salt and pepper to taste

1. Cook potatoes in a saucepan of boiling salted water until tender and drain. Return potatoes to saucepan and place over medium heat until dry, 1–3 minutes.
2. In food processor (or blender), add potatoes, garlic and onions. Process until all ingredients are finely chopped and blended.
3. In large skillet add enough oil to cover bottom of skillet (⅛ cup). Heat over medium-high heat and add mushrooms. Cook for 8 minutes until partially done. Remove and drain on paper towels.
4. In a large bowl, add ingredients (step 2) and diced cooked mushrooms (step 3) along with one small egg yolk and 1 cup of bread crumbs. Mix until pasty.
5. In a large skillet add olive oil (⅛ cup) and heat over medium heat. Beat 2 eggs in one bowl, and place bread crumbs in a second bowl. Take one spoonful of mixture (step 4) and dredge into the egg bowl and then into the bread crumb bowl.
6. In preheated skillet, place breaded spoonful and begin frying over medium heat. Cook about 5 fritters at a time. Cook for 3–4 minutes, turning once until golden brown on each side. Remove and drain on paper towels.
7. Preheat oven to 150°F. Place cooked batches in the oven, to keep warm until served. When last batch is done, arrange all the fritters on a platter. Serve immediately.

SERVES 6–8.

APPETIZERS, SOUPS & SUCH

Portabella Hash Browns

Ingredients:

⅛ cup olive oil

1 portabella mushroom, diced

½ medium onion, diced

3 medium brown raw potatoes,
  wash, peel, grate

  salt and pepper to taste

1. Wash, peel and grate potatoes in a large bowl.
2. Heat skillet, add oil to cover bottom of pan, and add diced mushrooms and onions. Cook over medium-high heat for 8 minutes, to partially cook the mushrooms.
3. Add cooked onions and mushrooms to the large bowl of grated raw potatoes. Scoop 3–4 large spoonfuls of mixture in a large skillet. Each potato patty will be approximately 3"×3"; brown on each side (golden-brown). Drain on paper towel.
4. Place cooked patties in 150ºF preheated oven covered with foil to keep warm, while continuing to cook 3–4 patties at a time on stovetop. When completed, remove patties from oven and arrange with last cooked batch. Serve immediately.

SERVES 6–8.

Portabella Turnover

Ingredients for Filling:

1	portabella mushroom, diced
1	small can corn, drained
4	green onions, chopped
2	medium potatoes, washed, peeled, diced
1	serrano pepper chopped, seeded
½	cup monterey jack cheese or mozzarella cheese, grated
1	tsp. paprika
⅛	cup olive oil (for skillet) vegetable oil for frying turnovers

1. Boil peeled potatoes until tender (20–40 minutes). Remove and dice. In large skillet at medium-high heat add enough olive oil to cover bottom of pan. Add mushrooms and cook for 15 minutes until moisture is reduced. Add cooked potatoes, onion, corn, serrano pepper and paprika and cook for an additional 5 minutes. Add cheese and remove.

Ingredients for Pastry:

1⅔	cup flour
7	tbsp. unsalted butter, melted
2–3	tbsp. water
½	tsp. salt

1. In a large bowl sift flour. Add salt, melted butter and water. Mix until semi-firm. On a floured board or marble top, knead until flexible and elastic. Cover with plastic wrap 30 minutes at room temperature.
2. On a floured surface, roll out dough to ⅛-inch thick and cut out rounds approximately 5 inches in diameter (approximately 14–16 rounds).
3. Fill each circular mound with 2–4 tablespoons of filling (see above). Coat edges of circle with water, fold circle in half and seal by crimping edges with finger. Refrigerate for 20–40 minutes prior to deep frying.
4. In a large pot, heat vegetable oil to high heat. Add one or two turnovers at a time. Deep fry until golden brown. Remove and drain on paper towels. Serve immediately.

SERVES 6–8.

Cream of Mushroom Soup with Sherry

Ingredients:

1	small to medium onion, diced
2–3	portabella mushrooms, thinly sliced
1	tbsp. unsalted butter
1	cup water
1	cup heavy cream
1	ounce medium-dry sherry
2	tbsp. chives, thinly sliced
	salt and pepper to taste

1. Cook diced onion and sliced mushrooms in a heavy saucepan with butter over medium-high heat until moisture has evaporated from the mushrooms and the onions are transparent, approximately 10–15 minutes.
2. In same saucepan, add water and cream and simmer for 15 minutes. In a blender, puree half the cooked mixture (mushrooms/onions/cream broth).
3. Add the puree to a soup pot and stir. Add the other half of the cooked ingredients and stir. Add sherry and salt and pepper to taste. Heat until hot and stir in chives. Serve immediately.

SERVES 2.

Creamy Mushroom Soup

Ingredients:

1	large onion, diced
⅛	cup butter/olive oil for sauté
3	tbsp. flour
1	cup milk
1	cup chicken broth
	(Option: vegetable broth)
1	cup of peas
4	large carrots
10	portabella mushrooms, diced
1	cup half and half
⅛	cup parsley
	salt and pepper to taste

1. Heat skillet and sauté the onions in butter or oil until transparent and golden in color. Set aside.
2. In another saucepan, create thickening mixture by sautéing flour in a small amount of butter over medium heat until brown, then slowly pouring milk into pan.
3. In a large pot add remaining ingredients (chicken broth, peas, carrots, parsley, mushrooms and half and half). Add thickening sauce (step 2) and sautéed onions (step 1). Cook over low heat for 1 to 1½ hours.
4. Pour all the ingredients into blender. Puree. Then, pour back into soup pot. Serve immediately.

SERVES 6.

Vegetable and Mushroom Soup

Ingredients:

1	quart water, or chicken or vegetable broth
2	tbsp. unsalted butter
4	portabella mushrooms, thinly sliced
2	large onions, diced
6	large cloves garlic, minced
4	medium carrots, peeled, diced
1	pound celery root, peeled, diced
4	medium potatoes peeled, diced

1. Add water to large soup pot at medium-high heat.
2. In skillet, add butter and mushrooms. Cook over medium-high heat for 15 minutes, then add onions and garlic. Continue to cook until onions are transparent and beginning to brown.
3. To large soup pot, add carrots, celery root and potatoes. Then add skillet mixture and cook for 1 to 1½ hours until flavors blend. Serve immediately.

SERVES 4–6.

APPETIZERS, SOUPS & SUCH

Creamy White Corn

Soup with Mushrooms

Ingredients:

5	ears white corn
⅓	cup unsalted butter
2	portabella mushrooms, diced
1	medium white onion, chopped
1	cup whipping cream
2	cups water (chicken/vegetable broth)
	salt and pepper to taste
	paprika for color

1. Remove raw corn kernels from the cob and place in a bowl.
2. In large soup pot at medium-high heat, add butter. Add diced portabellas and cook for 15 minutes.
3. Reduce heat to medium, add onions and continue cooking until onions are transparent, about 5–8 minutes.
4. Stir in kernels and cook for another 5 minutes. Stir in cream and continue cooking for 10 minutes.
5. Add water or broth to creamy mixture. Simmer for about 10 minutes. Add salt and pepper to taste. Top each serving with paprika for color and taste.

SERVES 6–8.

Garlic Mashed Potatoes

Ingredients:

4	medium brown potatoes, scrubbed
⅛	cup olive oil
2	portabella mushrooms, diced
2	cloves minced garlic
2–3	tbsp. butter
⅛	cup whipping cream (or half and half)
	salt and pepper to taste
	*Optional Garnish: sour cream

1. Place scrubbed potatoes into a large pot of water, enough to cover potatoes. Boil for 30 minutes or until tender. Remove and drain.

2. Cover bottom of large skillet with olive oil. Heat large skillet over medium-high heat. Add mushrooms and sauté for 10 minutes until moisture is reduced. Add minced garlic and continue cooking for additional 5 minutes. Do not let garlic brown or it will become bitter. Remove immediately.

3. Peel potatoes and place in large bowl. Add butter and whipping cream. Either beat with electric mixer or by hand until all ingredients are well mixed and creamy. Add salt and pepper to taste.

4. Top each serving of mashed potatoes with sautéed mushrooms/garlic (ingredients from step 2). Serve immediately. As an optional garnish, top with a dollop of sour cream.

SERVES 4.

SALADS
&
VEGGIES

Portabellas with Dates and Walnuts

Ingredients:

⅛	cup olive oil
4	portabella mushrooms, diced
2	tsp. paprika
2	medium sweet onions, diced
1	cup dates, chopped
1	cup walnuts, chopped

1. Take large skillet and coat bottom with oil. Add mushrooms and cook over medium-high heat. Add 2 teaspoons paprika and cook for 10 minutes until moisture is reduced. Add diced onions and continue to cook for 5 minutes until transparent. Add dates and cook for 1–2 minutes more. Add walnuts and allow to warm for 1 minute. Serve immediately.

SERVES 4–6.

SALADS & VEGGIES

Portabella Salad

Ingredients:

⅔	cup olive oil
4	portabella mushrooms, diced
4	medium red and yellow fresh beets, diced*
1	medium celery root, peeled, diced
1	bunch green onions, chopped
1	cup cilantro, chopped
¼	cup crumbled feta cheese
2	tsp. balsamic vinegar
1	pinch African spice**
	salt to taste

1. In skillet add ⅛ cup of olive oil and cook half of diced mushrooms over medium-high heat for 15 minutes until moisture is reduced.
2. In large bowl toss cooked mushrooms and all other raw ingredients (including diced raw mushrooms), adding ⅛ cup olive oil and 2 teaspoons balsamic vinegar. Immediately serve in large shallow serving bowl.

SERVES 6.

*You cannot use canned beets for this recipe! Using both colored beets (red and yellow), adds variety and beautiful color to the overall final appearance of the dish.

**African spice is very fragrant and can be found in most specialty stores.

SALADS & VEGGIES

Grilled Portabella Salad

Ingredients for Dressing:

1	cup mayonnaise
2	tbsp. wine vinegar
2	tbsp. mustard
6	cloves garlic, minced
2	tsp. honey

Ingredients for Salad:

1	bunch fresh spinach, washed, torn leaves
2	tomatoes, chopped
⅓	cup chopped fresh rosemary
1	medium onion, sliced
4	portabella mushrooms, sliced
⅛	cup olive oil
1	cup croutons
	salt and pepper to taste

1. Dressing: Combine mayonnaise, vinegar, mustard, garlic and honey. Cover and chill until ready to serve.
2. Spinach mixture: In a large bowl, toss washed spinach, tomatoes, rosemary and onion. Cover and chill until ready to serve.
3. Take sliced mushrooms and coat with olive oil, salt and pepper.
4. Prepare grill. When ready, grill mushrooms for 5 minutes on each side, or to your liking.*Remove.
5. Cut the sliced BBQ'd mushrooms into bite-sized pieces.
6. Combine mushrooms, croutons and the spinach mixture in a bowl. Add chilled dressing. Toss until well coated. Serve immediately.

SERVES 4–6.

*Indoor grill may be used.

Green Salad with Mushrooms

Ingredients:

½ head butter lettuce (washed, torn leaves)

½ head romaine lettuce (washed, torn leaves)

¼ cup carrot, washed, peeled, grated

¼ cup red cabbage, raw, shredded

½ bell pepper, thinly sliced (green, orange or red)*

6–8 green onions, chopped

1 medium tomato, sliced

1 portabella mushroom, diced

Salad Dressing:

⅓ cup balsamic vinegar

1 cup olive oil

2 tsp. sugar

1 minced garlic clove

1 tsp. ketchup

½ tsp. onion powder

¼ tsp. salt

¼ tsp. pepper

1. Mix all ingredients in salad bowl. Cover and chill until ready to serve.
2. Shake or blend dressing in blender. Pour dressing over salad. Toss and serve.

SERVES 4.

*Use all three colored bell peppers to add variety and color to this dish.

Broccoli and Mushroom Salad

Ingredients:

½	bunch broccoli blossoms, washed, halved
2	portabella mushrooms, diced
1	medium tomato, sliced
6–8	green onions, chopped

Salad Dressing:

¼	cup balsamic vinegar
⅔	cup olive oil
2	tsp. sugar
1	tsp. ketchup
½	tsp. mustard
½	tsp. garlic, minced

1. In a large salad bowl add: broccoli blossoms, portabella mushrooms, tomato and green onions. Chill until ready to serve.
2. Mix dressing. Remove chilled salad from refrigerator. Pour dressing on salad. Toss until evenly coated and serve.

SERVES 4.

Greek Salad

Ingredients:

1–2	portabella mushrooms, stemmed, diced
1	large tomato, or 2 medium tomatoes, diced
1	red onion, diced
1	cucumber, diced
2	oz. feta cheese
	Greek olives*
	Greek salad dressing

1. Toss mushrooms, tomatoes, onion, cucumber and olives then toss them in a bowl.
2. Cut the feta cheese into small bite-sized squares, toss in same bowl (step 1).
3. Add Greek salad dressing, tossing as you pour. Serve immediately.

*Traditional Greek olives come with pits in them! You can choose black or green Greek olives; whole or halved Greek olives.

Tomato, Basil and Mozzarella Salad

Ingredients:

2	tomatoes, sliced*
2	portabella mushrooms, diced
6	sprigs of fresh basil, washed, torn
	fresh mozzarella cheese, sliced**
1	small red onion, sliced
⅛	cup balsamic vinegar
⅔	cup olive oil
	garlic croutons

1. Place tomatoes, mushrooms, basil and mozzarella cheese on a large serving platter. Top with red onion slices and garlic croutons. Drizzle with balsamic vinegar and olive oil.

SERVES 6.

*Use 1 red tomato and 1 yellow if in season. This adds variety, color and taste to this dish.

**Fresh mozzarella can be found in specialty grocery stores. If you cannot find fresh, commercial grade mozzarella is adequate.

SALADS & VEGGIES

Cucumber, Red Onion and Mango Salad

Ingredients:

1	cucumber*, diced
1	medium red onion, diced
2	portabella mushrooms, diced
1	mango, diced
¼	bunch cilantro, washed, stemmed, chopped
	lime juice
	salt to taste

1. Take salad bowl and add the following: cucumber, mushrooms, mango and red onion.
2. Drizzle with lime juice. Season lightly with salt. Toss. Sprinkle individual servings with chopped cilantro as garnish. Serve immediately or chill until ready to serve.

SERVES 4–6.

*Use English or pickling cucumbers because they are sweeter.

Red Onion, Red Pepper and Tomato Salad

Ingredients:

1	portabella mushroom (very thinly sliced, almost julienne)
¼	red onion, thinly sliced
½	red bell pepper, thinly sliced
1	medium tomato, sliced

Ingredients for Dressing:

⅛	cup balsamic vinegar
⅔	cup olive oil
2	tsp. minced garlic
1	tsp. ketchup
2	tsp. sugar
¼	tsp. mustard
¼	tsp. dried onion

1. Mix salad dressing.
2. Place salad ingredients in a large salad bowl. Pour dressing over ingredients and toss until evenly coated. Serve immediately.

SERVES 4–6.

Mandarin Orange and Portabella Salad

Ingredients:

1	head butter lettuce, washed, torn
1	medium red onion, sliced
1	sliced avocado
1	portabella mushroom, diced
1	can mandarin orange slices, drained (save juice for dressing)

Poppy Seed Dressing:

4–6	tbsp. mandarin orange juice from can
1	tbsp. sugar—or more to taste
1	tsp. dry mustard
½	tsp. salt
⅓	cup white wine vinegar
2	tbsp. onion, grated
1	cup olive oil
2	tbsp. poppy seeds

1. Prepare salad: Add lettuce (washed and torn leaves) in a bowl, then add onion, avocado, portabella mushroom and mandarin orange pieces. Chill.
2. Using a whisk, mix salad dressing starting with first five ingredients (mandarin orange juice, sugar, mustard, salt, vinegar). Slowly add last three ingredients (onion, oil, poppy seeds).*
3. Remove salad from refrigerator. Pour dressing over chilled salad. Toss until all items are evenly coated. Serve immediately.

Serves 4.

*You may use a blender if you prefer.

SALADS & VEGGIES

Veggie Quiche

Ingredients:

4	eggs
1½	cups half and half
1	tsp. basil
¼	tsp. pepper to taste
1	clove garlic, minced
1	portabella mushroom, diced
1	carrot, diced
½	bunch fresh spinach (washed, stemmed, torn leaves)
1	cup shredded Swiss or Gruyere cheese

Pastry Crust:

2¼	cups flour
½	tsp. salt
¾	cup shortening
4–5	tbsp. cold water

1. Pastry shell: Stir flour and salt in a large bowl. Cut in shortening with a knife. Blend, then mix in cold water until dough forms a ball and comes clean from side of bowl. Sprinkle flour on a flat work surface (wood or marble). Divide dough ball in half. Wrap each half in plastic and refrigerate for 1 hour.

2. With rolling pin on floured work surface, roll one dough ball* into a round shape. Place dough crust onto pie tin. Pierce with fork. Cover with foil and baked in preheated oven at 450ºF for 10 minutes. Remove from oven and let cool.

3. Mix eggs, half and half, basil, pepper and garlic in a large bowl. Fold in mushrooms, onions, carrot and spinach. Pour into prebaked pastry shell. Top with cheese.

4. Bake in preheated oven at 325ºF for 35–40 minutes or until knife comes out clean. Let stand 5–10 minutes before serving.

Serves 6.

*Only half the dough is needed for this recipe. Either roll out the second half of the dough and freeze the pie crust for future use or freeze the dough in bulk for next time.

Portabella and Onion Crepes

Ingredients for Crepes:

½	cup flour
½	cup milk
¼	cup water
2	large eggs
2	tbsp. melted butter
1	pinch of salt

Ingredients for Filling:

⅛	cup olive oil
2	tbsp. butter
2	portabella mushroom, diced
1	large onion, diced
	salt and pepper to taste

Ingredients for Cooking:

2	tbsp. butter (cooking mushrooms/onions)
1/8	cup olive oil (cooking mushrooms/onions)
4–6	tbsp. butter (cooking crepes)

1. Filling: Cover bottom of skillet with olive oil and 2 tablespoons of butter and heat over medium-high heat. Add mushrooms and sauté for 10 minutes until moisture is reduced. Add the diced onion and salt and pepper to taste. Continue cooking for 5 minutes more, until onions are transparent and golden. Remove immediately.

2. Crepes: In blender or food processor (or by hand with a whisk), blend: flour, milk, water, eggs, butter and salt. Whip into creamy batter. Heat a 6-inch crepe pan or a flat pan. Brush bottom of pan with melted butter, pour in ⅛ cup of batter until pan bottom is covered with a thin layer of batter. Cook over medium heat until top is opaque—then flip or turn crepe and continue cooking. Place in warm oven when done. Continue process with remaining batter until 8 crepes are made.

3. Fill each crepe with 2–3 tablespoons of mushroom/onion mixture. Roll crepe and place foldside down on platter. Serve immediately.

SERVES 4–8.

Hot Eggplant with Mushrooms

Ingredients:

⅛	cup sesame seed oil
1	portabella mushroom, diced
2–3	tbsp. chicken broth
3	cloves garlic, minced
1	medium onion, diced
1	eggplant, peeled, diced
⅛	cup tamari sauce (available in local grocery store, or specialty store)
⅛	tsp. dried red chili peppers
	*Garnish: roasted sesame seeds

1. Heat skillet or wok over medium-high heat. Add oil to cover bottom of pan and add mushrooms. Cook for 15 minutes. Remove mushrooms to a bowl.

2. In the same skillet, cook: chicken broth, garlic and onion for 2–3 minutes.

3. Add eggplant and return cooked mushrooms to the wok or skillet. Continue cooking for another 5 minutes. Finally, add tamari sauce and chili peppers. Stir quickly. Remove from skillet. Serve as entree or side dish, garnished with sesame seeds if desired. Serve immediately.

Serves 4.

Caesar Salad with Mushrooms

Ingredients:

1	head Romaine lettuce, washed, torn
1	portabella mushroom, diced
	garlic croutons
	parmesan cheese

Ingredients for Caesar Dressing:

1	egg yolk (if desired)
5–7	anchovies
1	clove garlic, cut in half
¼	cup olive oil
2	tbsp. lemon juice
2	tbsp. parmesan cheese
1½	tsp. Worcestershire sauce
⅓	tsp. ground pepper

1. In a blender, add all the ingredients for dressing and blend. Keep at room temperature when ready to serve.
2. Place torn Romaine leaves in a large salad bowl. Pour Caesar dressing over the lettuce and toss until leaves are well coated. Add mushrooms and croutons and toss again until evenly coated. Sprinkle parmesan cheese on top of salad before serving. Serve immediately.

SERVES 4–6.

Sautéed with Crimini Mushrooms

Ingredients:

1	pound portabella mushrooms, remove stems
1	pound crimini mushrooms
3	large shallots
1	stick (½ cup) butter, unsalted
¼	cup balsamic vinegar
5	tbsp. soy sauce
½	cup sugar
4	scallions (green stems only), diagonally cut into thin slices
	salt and pepper to taste

1. Cut portabellas and criminis into 1-inch slices.
2. Chop shallots and add butter to large skillet. Cook over moderate heat, stirring, for 1 minute. Add portabellas, salt and pepper to taste. Cook, stirring occasionally for 5 minutes. Add crimini mushrooms and cook for another 10 minutes, stirring occasionally, until liquid is evaporated.
3. In a bowl whisk together: vinegar, soy sauce and sugar. Add to cooked mushrooms. Boil mixture for 3 minutes, or until liquid is reduced slightly. Stir in scallions at the last minute. Serve immediately.

SERVES 8.

SALADS & VEGGIES

Spicy Corn and Onions

Ingredients:

⅛	cup olive oil
1	portabella mushroom, diced
3–5	tbsp. sweet butter
1	tsp. garlic, minced
1	medium onion, diced
1	tsp. ground cumin
1	tsp. ground coriander
2	dried red chilies, crushed
1	serrano pepper, diced
1	Mexican red pepper, diced
1	can corn kernels, drained
	fresh cilantro, washed, chopped
	salt to taste

1. Heat skillet. Add olive oil to cover bottom of pan and add mushrooms. Cook at medium-high heat for 15 minutes. Remove immediately.
2. In separate skillet, melt butter and add: garlic, onion, cumin, coriander, dried red chilies, serrano, Mexican pepper, salt, corn and cooked mushrooms. Cook for approximately 5–7 minutes, until all flavors blend. Serve immediately. Garnish with fresh cilantro.

SERVES 4.

SALADS & VEGGIES

Portabella Mexican Salad

Ingredients:

⅛	cup olive oil
1	portabella mushroom, diced
2	cups kernels of canned corn
1	red bell pepper, diced
1	yellow bell pepper, diced
½	cup cooked black beans (or 1 can)
1	jalapeno chili, minced
1	red onion, diced
½	cup cilantro, chopped
1	tbsp. minced fresh ginger
½	tsp. of sugar (to taste)
½	lime (squeeze juice)
	salt to taste

1. Cover bottom of large skillet with olive oil. Add mushrooms and cook over medium-high heat. Stir occasionally, until liquid from mushrooms is evaporated, about 10–15 minutes.
2. Place kernels of canned corn in a large bowl. If you choose to use fresh ears of corn, take two ears of corn and roast over grill. Take corn off the grill and cut the kernels off the cob with a sharp knife. Place corn kernels in a large bowl.
3. Add the following to the corn: cooked mushrooms, red and yellow bell pepper, cooked black beans, jalapeno, red onion, cilantro, ginger, sugar and lime juice. Salt to taste. Toss until well mixed. Serve immediately.

SERVES 4–6.

Summer Squash with
Garlic and Mushrooms

Ingredients:

2	yellow crookneck squash, sliced
2	small green zucchini, sliced
2	small yellow zucchini, sliced
⅛	cup olive oil
2	portabella mushrooms, sliced
1	clove minced garlic
1	medium yellow onion, sliced
1	tbsp. basil
	salt and pepper to taste

1. Wash, trim and slice all squash. If you prefer, you can cut them julienne style (thin slivers).
2. Cover bottom of large skillet lightly with olive oil. Over medium-high heat add sliced mushrooms and cook for 15 minutes until moisture is reduced. Add squash, garlic and onion and continue cooking for 5–8 minutes until squash begins to brown and onions become transparent. Do not overcook squash! Add basil, salt and pepper to taste. Serve immediately.

SERVES 6–8.

GRILLED
& STUFFED

BBQ with Veggies

Ingredients:

(all vegetables should be in ½"-thick slices)

1	red bell pepper, sliced
1	green bell pepper, sliced
2	small green zucchini, sliced
2	small yellow zucchini, sliced
2	portabella mushrooms, sliced
4–6	green onions, whole
	olive oil and balsamic vinegar
	spices to taste
	*Option: minced garlic, 2 tsp.
	sugar

1. Place washed, sliced vegetables/mushrooms in a large bowl. Marinate with balsamic vinegar and olive oil dressing, adding optional spices to taste. Let sit for 30 minutes, turning every 10 minutes to ensure proper coating.
2. Place vegetables and mushrooms on hot BBQ grill. Cook for 15 minutes. Using tongs, turn and continue grilling for another 15 minutes.
3. When done serve immediately.

SERVES 6–8.

Note: If preferred, after properly marinating, skewer all the vegetables/mushrooms, alternating each vegetable on the skewer. Grill by rotating skewer every 5 minutes.

GRILLED & STUFFED

Grilled with Asparagus

Ingredients:

¼	cup balsamic vinegar
¾	cup olive oil
2	tbsp. chopped onion
3	cloves garlic, minced
1	tsp. fresh basil
1	tsp. lemon pepper
½	tsp. salt
1	tbsp. sugar
3	portabella mushrooms, cut into one-inch strips
2	pounds asparagus, washed, snap ends

1. Combine: vinegar, oil, onion, garlic, basil, lemon pepper, salt and sugar in a bowl. Mix well. Place the mixture in a gallon plastic storage bag with the mushrooms and asparagus, turning to coat all the ingredients. Let the mixture marinate in the refrigerator for at least 30 minutes, turning the bag a few times during marinating.
2. Place asparagus and strips of mushrooms onto a hot grill (or under broiler), reserving marinade. Turn after 20 minutes or when brown and cooked to your taste (longer for softer).
3. When done, plate mushrooms and top with asparagus. Pour 3–4 teaspoons of marinade over the vegetables. Serve immediately.

SERVES 3–4.

GRILLED & STUFFED

Grilled Whole/Lox

Ingredients:

2	whole portabella mushrooms, remove stems
¼	pound lox
1	4 oz. block of cream cheese, sliced
4	tbsp. olive oil
	capers

1. Coat mushrooms evenly with olive oil.
2. When coals on grill are gray and ready, place each mushroom gill side down on grill and cook on each side for 15 minutes for a total of 30 minutes. Grill will be hot and you must watch mushrooms as the olive oil will make the grill flame. Cover grill with lid until flame subsides (if needed). Remove and place on plate, gill side down.
3. Top each grilled portabella with lox (as many slices as you want). Top with a slice of cream cheese and capers. Serve immediately.

SERVES 2.

GRILLED & STUFFED

Grilled/BBQ Sauce

Ingredients:

4	portabella mushrooms, sliced
1	cup BBQ sauce
6–8	tbsp. olive oil

1. Place sliced portabella mushrooms in a large bowl. Add olive oil. Toss until each slice is well coated.

2. Pour BBQ sauce into a medium-size bowl. Have a basting brush ready to baste the mushrooms.

3. When coals on grill are gray and ready, place each mushroom slice on grill and cook for 15 minutes. Turn with tongs and continue to cook for 15 minutes. Grill will be hot and you must watch mushrooms as the olive oil will make the grill flame. Cover grill with lid until flame subsides (if needed).

4. After you have cooked the mushrooms once on each side, baste with BBQ sauce on both sides. Turn slices quickly for 2–3 minutes to avoid burning. Serve immediately as an hors d'oeuvre or as side dish to main course. Or place mushrooms between slices of bread to make a sandwich.

SERVES 4–6.

Tomato Bruschetta

Ingredients:

4	tomatoes, chopped
8	sprigs fresh basil, rinsed, dried, chopped
2	portabella mushrooms, sliced one-inch thick
2	garlic cloves, minced
3	tbsp. olive oil
2	slices crusty Italian/French bread

1. In a bowl mix chopped tomatoes and fresh chopped basil together.

2. In a large skillet heat 2 tablespoons oil over moderate heat until hot but not smoking. Cook mushrooms and garlic with salt and pepper to taste. Stir until liquid is evaporated, about 10 minutes. Remove skillet from heat and toss mushrooms with remaining tablespoon of oil. Keep mushrooms warm, covered in a separate bowl.

3. Toast bread. Scoop tomato/basil mixture (step 1) on top of bread. Scoop cooked portabellas on top of tomato/basil mixture. Serve immediately.

SERVES 4.

Quick Stuffed Eggplant

Ingredients:

1	medium eggplant, halved
⅛	cup olive oil
2	portabella mushrooms, diced
½	medium white or yellow onion, diced

1. Wash eggplant under cool water and pat dry, then slice in half. Take a large spoon and scrape out the eggplant seeds. The meat of the eggplant should be seedless.
2. In a skillet, cover the bottom of pan with olive oil. Heat over medium-high heat. Add mushrooms and sauté for 10 minutes. Add onions and cook with mushrooms for 5 more minutes until onions are transparent.
3. Take large spoonfuls of sautéed onions and mushrooms and scoop into the inside of the raw eggplant.
4. Heat oven to 350°F and place eggplant halves side by side on cookie sheet to cook until brown, 15–20 minutes. Serve immediately.

SERVES 2.

GRILLED & STUFFED

Skewered with Teriyaki Sauce

Ingredients:

2	portabella mushrooms, chunks
¼	cup of your favorite teriyaki sauce
12	metal (or wooden) skewers

1. Slide mushrooms onto skewers, one large chunk at a time, until skewer is filled.
2. Pour teriyaki in a medium bowl, for basting.
3. Place mushrooms over hot BBQ grill for 5 minutes. Turn and cook for another 5 minutes (total of 10 minutes).
4. Brush teriyaki sauce over mushrooms on both sides until coated. Continue to cook for another 3–5 minutes, turning frequently to avoid burning. The sugar in the teriyaki sauce can cause the mushroom to burn quickly. When done serve immediately.

SERVES 6–8.

GRILLED & STUFFED

Stuffed Portabellas

Ingredients:

2	whole portabella mushrooms, remove stems
4	tbsp. olive oil
1	cup bread crumbs
¼	cup parmesan cheese, grated
1	tbsp. chopped fresh parsley
1	small tomato, diced
	*Option: cilantro in place of parsley, cayenne pepper or other spices

1. Preheat broiler. Remove stems and clean mushrooms. Mushrooms will all have a small cavity after stem is removed.
2. In a large bowl, mix together: bread crumbs, cheese, parsley, tomato and salt and pepper to taste.
3. Place mushrooms stem side down. Brush top and bottom of whole mushrooms with olive oil. Broil mushrooms 5–7 minutes close to the heat until golden. Turn mushrooms over and season with salt and pepper. Broil 5–7 minutes more.
4. Spoon the bread crumb-mixture onto the center of the broiled mushrooms and spread evenly, then drizzle with a little olive oil. Broil until golden brown, 1–3 minutes. Keep a close eye on them and remove them as soon as they turn golden brown. Serve immediately.

SERVES 2.

Stuffed Bell Pepper

Ingredients:

⅛	cup olive oil
3	portabella mushrooms, diced
4	cloves garlic, minced
1	medium onion, diced
4	medium bell peppers (green, orange or red)
¼	cup fresh parsley, minced
½	cup parmesan cheese, grated

1. Take skillet and cover bottom with olive oil. Over medium-high heat add mushrooms and cook for 10 minutes. Add onions and garlic and cook for 5 minutes until onions are transparent. (If garlic turns brown, it is overcooked and it will become bitter.) Remove mushroom/onion/garlic mixture and place in bowl when done.
2. Cut off top of bell peppers (to make a hat) and remove inside seeds and membrane. Wash and drain.
3. In separate bowl mix together cooked mushrooms, sautéed onions/garlic, fresh parsley and parmesan cheese.
4. Stuff each bell pepper to the top with all mixed ingredients. Replace hat (lid) of bell pepper and bake at 425°F in preheated oven for 20–25 minutes. Remove from oven. Serve immediately.

SERVES 4.

Grilled Polenta

Ingredients:

1	package of polenta
⅛	cup olive oil
8	oz. mozzarella cheese, sliced
3–4	tbsp. butter
2	portabella mushrooms, diced
1	can chicken broth
¼	cup port wine

1. In large skillet add butter and mushrooms. Cook over medium-high heat for 15 minutes. Remove mushrooms when done. In same skillet, add chicken broth and port wine. Cook over high heat until liquid is reduced by half. Return mushrooms to same skillet in reduced broth and keep warm.

2. Slice polenta ¼-inch thick. In a separate skillet, cover bottom of skillet with olive oil. Cook sliced polenta over medium-high heat. After turning once, place a slice of fresh mozzarella cheese on top of each slice of polenta. Continue cooking until cheese melts (approximately 4 minutes).

3. Serve each slice of cooked polenta (with melted cheese) topped with mushroom/wine mixture. Serve immediately.

SERVES 6.

GRILLED & STUFFED

Classic Cajun Grilled

Ingredients:

4   portabella mushrooms, sliced
one-inch thick

6–8   tbsp. olive oil
Cajun seasoning

1. Place sliced portabella mushrooms in large bowl. Add olive oil and Cajun seasoning. Toss until each slice is well coated.
2. Continue to toss every 15 minutes for 30–45 minutes prior to grilling. If mushrooms become dry add more olive oil to coat each mushroom. Do not saturate with oil, only lightly coat with the olive oil. Continue to add Cajun spice every time you recoat with oil every 15 minutes.
3. When coals on grill are gray and ready, place each mushroom slice on grill. Cook for 5 minutes. Turn mushrooms and cook 5 minutes more. Grill will be hot; you must watch mushrooms as the oil will make the grill flame. Cover grill with lid until flame subsides (if needed). Serve immediately as hors d'oeuvre or as a side dish.

SERVES 4–6.

GRILLED & STUFFED

Grilled with Thick Creamy Polenta

Ingredients:

1	12-oz package of polenta (can be found in local grocery store)
¼	cup half and half, or whipping cream
1	pound of mozzarella, grated
4	tbsp. olive oil, used for coating mushrooms
4	whole portabella mushrooms, remove stems
⅛	cup olive oil
1	medium yellow onion, diced

1. In a large saucepan, combine polenta, cream and mozzarella. Cook over low heat until it becomes one creamy (not runny) mixture. Stir frequently.
2. Coat each mushroom with 1 tablespoon olive oil until well coated.
3. Cover bottom of large skillet with olive oil and over medium heat, add diced onions. Sauté until onions are transparent, approximately 7 minutes.
4. Grilling: When coals are gray and ready, place each mushroom gill side down on grill. Cook for 15 minutes. Turn with tongs and cook another 15 minutes. Remove mushrooms from grill.
5. Coat each plate with a large spoonful of creamy polenta mixture. Place each cooked mushroom over the creamy polenta mixture. Top with a dollop of sautéed onions. Serve immediately.

SERVES 4.

GRILLED & STUFFED

Stuffed Tomatoes

Ingredients:

⅓	cup olive oil
2	portabella mushrooms, diced
1	medium onion, diced
4	cloves garlic, minced
4	medium tomatoes
¼	cup fresh parsley, minced
½	cup parmesan cheese, grated

1. Take skillet and cover bottom with olive oil. Over medium-high heat add mushrooms and cook for 10 minutes. Add onions and garlic and cook for 5 minutes until onions are transparent. (If garlic turns brown, it is overcooked and it will become bitter.) Remove and place in bowl when done.
2. Cut off end of tomatoes and remove inside seeds and membrane. Drain.
3. In separate bowl mix together cooked mushrooms, sautéed onions and garlic, fresh parsley and parmesan cheese.
4. Stuff tomatoes to the top with all ingredients, and bake at 375°F in preheated oven for 20–25 minutes. Remove from oven and serve immediately.

Serves 4.

GRILLED & STUFFED

Stuffed Baked Potato

Ingredients:

4	medium brown potatoes, scrubbed
⅛	cup olive oil
2	portabella mushrooms, diced
1	medium onion, diced
2–3	tbsp. butter
⅛	cup whipping cream (or half and half)
	salt and pepper to taste
	*Optional Garnish: sour cream

1. Cover potatoes with olive oil. Pierce with fork. Bake in preheated oven at 400ºF for 1 hour.
2. Cover bottom of skillet with olive oil. Heat large skillet over medium-high heat. Add mushrooms and sauté for 10 minutes until moisture is reduced. Add onion and continue cooking for 5 more minutes until onions are transparent and golden. Remove immediately.
3. When potatoes are done, remove from oven. Halve potatoes and scoop out the insides into a large bowl. Leave potato skins on baking dish. To potato mixture add butter and a minimum amount of whipping cream. Beat with electric mixer (or beat by hand) until creamy. Add salt and pepper to taste.
4. When blended, take one scoop of whipped potato mixture and begin to fill inside of potato skin. Then sequentially take a scoop of mushroom and onion mixture and place inside the potato skin. Continue alternating potato and mushroom mixture until the potato is stuffed above skin line with filling. Serve immediately. As optional garnish top with a dollop of sour cream.

SERVES 4.

GRILLED & STUFFED

Mushroom Stuffed Eggplant

Ingredients:

4	small eggplants
⅛	cup olive oil
2	portabella mushrooms, diced
1	medium onion, diced
1	clove minced garlic
½	tsp. thyme
1	tbsp. basil
½	cup parmesan cheese, grated
2	eggs, beaten
¼	cup butter
1	cup bread crumbs

1. Wash and scrub eggplants. Halve the eggplants lengthwise, hollow out, and cut the flesh into small cubes. Outer skin should be ½- inch thick.
2. Take large skillet and cover bottom of pan with olive oil. Over medium-high heat cook mushrooms for 10 minutes. Add onions, garlic and eggplant cubes and cook for another 5–7 minutes until onions are transparent. Remove immediately.
3. In a large bowl, mix sautéed onions, garlic, eggplant cubes and mushrooms (step 2) with the following: thyme, basil, ¼ cup parmesan cheese and eggs. Stir.
4. Preheat oven to 425ºF and grease baking dish. Place hollowed eggplant halves in baking dish. Fill each with mixture from step 3. Top with remaining bread crumbs, parmesan cheese and pat of butter. Bake for 20–25 minutes until golden brown. Remove and serve immediately.

Serves 4.

Stuffed Zucchini

Ingredients:

4	large zucchini
⅛	cup olive oil
2	portabella mushrooms, diced
1	medium onion, diced
1	clove minced garlic
½	tsp. thyme
1	tbsp. basil
½	cup parmesan cheese, grated
2	eggs, beaten
1	cup bread crumbs
¼	cup butter

1. Wash, scrub and halve the zucchini lengthwise. Hollow out and cut the flesh into small cubes.

2. Take large skillet and cover bottom of pan with olive oil. Over medium-high heat cook mushrooms for 10 minutes. Add onions, garlic and zucchini and cook for 5–7 minutes until onions are transparent. Remove immediately.

3. Mix sautéed onions, garlic, zucchini cubes and mushrooms (step 2) with the following: thyme, basil, ¼ cup parmesan cheese and eggs. Stir together in large bowl.

4. Preheat oven to 425ºF and grease baking dish. Place zucchini halves in baking dish. Fill with mixture from step 3. Top with remaining bread crumbs, parmesan cheese and a pat of butter. Bake for 20–25 minutes until golden brown. Remove and serve immediately.

SERVES 4.

FROM LAND
TO SEA

FROM LAND TO SEA

Steak and Portabellas

Ingredients:

⅛	cup olive oil
4–6	portabella mushrooms, sliced
2	tbsp. sage
4	beef rib eye steaks
2	tbsp. coarsely ground pepper
	salt to taste

1. Take large skillet and cover bottom of pan with oil. Over medium-high heat, add mushrooms and sage. Cook until moisture is reduced, approximately 15 minutes. Remove immediately.
2. Coat both sides of rib eye steaks evenly with ground pepper. Grill over hot coals until done to your liking. Remove from grill.
3. Top each with cooked mushrooms and serve on separate plates.

SERVES 4.

FROM LAND TO SEA

Flamed Steak

Ingredients:

2	portabella mushrooms, cubed
½	tbsp. Worcestershire sauce
2	tbsp. brandy or cognac
24	small white pearl onions, peeled
6–8	tbsp. olive oil
1	pound steak of your choice, trimmed, cubed*
	salt and pepper to taste

1. Coat bottom of skillet with olive oil and add mushrooms. Cook for 10 or more minutes until moisture is reduced. Add Worcestershire sauce and brandy while cooking. Add pearl onions and cook for another 5–7 minutes until tender and transparent.
2. Pour remaining olive oil into a second skillet and heat to medium-high. Brown steak on all sides until done to your liking (rare, medium rare or well done).
3. When steaks are done, pour mushroom/onion/brandy mixture over the top of the steaks and serve immediately.

*Avoid any steak with bones for this recipe.

SERVES 2–4.

Turkey Chili with Portabellas

Ingredients:

⅛	cup olive oil
2	portabella mushrooms, diced
2	pounds ground turkey (or beef if preferred)
3–4	cloves minced garlic
2	medium onions, diced
1	tbsp. chili powder
½	tsp. cumin
1	tsp. salt
3+	medium tomatoes, chopped
1	tbsp. flour
1	cup water (or more if needed)

1. In large skillet, at medium-high heat, cover bottom with olive oil and add ground meat. Sauté for 10–15 minutes or until browned. Remove.
2. In large skillet, at medium-high heat, add oil and cook mushrooms for 15 minutes.
3. To mushroom skillet, add garlic, onions, chili powder, cumin and salt. Stir and continue cooking for another 5 minutes, then add cooked meat (step1). Stir and cook for 1–2 minutes so that both meat and mushrooms are spiced evenly.
4. Add chopped tomatoes, flour and water to skillet. Mixture will be soupy. Let cook over low heat for approximately ½ hour, stirring every 10 minutes until reduced. Serve in bowls when done.

SERVES 8.

Chicken with Mushroom Sauce

Ingredients:

⅛	cup olive oil
4	chicken breasts, halved
1–2	tbsp. butter
2	tbsp. flour
¼	tsp. salt
¼	tsp. pepper
1	can chicken broth (or vegetable broth)
4	portabella mushrooms, sliced
3–4	green onions, chopped

1. In skillet, cook olive oil over medium-high heat. Place chicken breasts in skillet and cook for 10–15 minutes until golden brown and done (if it is pink in the middle it is uncooked). Remove chicken breasts. Use this same skillet with chicken drippings to make sauce in step 2.

2. Add butter to chicken drippings over medium heat. Add: flour, salt and pepper, stirring constantly (until flour turns a golden brown). Do not burn flour! Slowly add chicken broth to browned flour. Stir until thickened. If necessary, add flour to thicken.

3. Over medium-high heat cover bottom of second skillet with olive oil. Cook sliced mushrooms until moisture is reduced (about 15 minutes). When done remove portabellas from skillet and add to the sauce in step 2. Finally, add chopped green onions to sauce. The heat of the sauce will cook and soften the green onions.

4. Place chicken breasts on serving platter and pour portabella mushroom sauce over the chicken. Serve immediately with rice.

SERVES 4.

FROM LAND TO SEA

Portabella and Asparagus
Stuffed Chicken Breasts

Ingredients:

8	chicken breasts, boned, skinned and halved
16	small fresh asparagus spears, washed, trimmed
8	slices of mozzarella cheese (fresh if preferred—can be found in specialty stores)
4	portabella mushrooms, sliced
3	eggs, well beaten
2	cups bread crumbs
½	cup butter
	salt and pepper to taste

1. Preheat oven to 350ºF. Lay out chicken on cutting board between 2 pieces of plastic wrap. Flatten chicken with rolling pin.
2. Wash and snap ends of asparagus off by holding asparagus at each end and bending until it naturally snaps. Discard thicker bottom end. Slice fresh mozzarella cheese into 4 even ⅛" slices.
3. Place 2 asparagus spears, 2 slices of mushrooms and one slice of mozzarella cheese on each flattened chicken breast. (Add salt and pepper if desired.) Fold chicken over filling and secure with wooden toothpicks.
4. Beat eggs with wire wisk. Dip rolled chicken into beaten egg mixture, then coat with bread crumbs.
5. Heat skillet over medium heat and melt butter. Add chicken to skillet and cook for 6–8 minutes on each side until golden brown. Remove chicken and place on a baking sheet or in a glass baking dish (9" × 12"). Place in heated oven and cook for 15–20 minutes or until golden brown. Serve immediately.

SERVES 8.

FROM LAND TO SEA

Lamb Chops and Gravy

Ingredients:

⅛	cup olive oil
4	lamb chops
2–4	tbsp. flour
4	portabella mushrooms, diced
¼	cup water
	salt and pepper to taste

1. Cover bottom of skillet with olive oil and cook lamb chops over medium to high heat until done to your liking. Remove chops.
2. Keep warm by covering with foil and putting in warm preheated oven at 150°F until ready to use. Make gravy by pouring ¼ cup water and whisk brown bits loose; add flour and continue stirring until roux is browned over medium-high heat. Stir until thickened.
3. In a separate skillet, cover bottom with olive oil. Add mushrooms and cook over medium to high heat for 15 minutes until moisture is reduced.
4. Remove chops from oven. Serve lamb chops and portabellas on a platter. Top with gravy. Serve immediately.

SERVES 4.

FROM LAND TO SEA

Chicken or Beef Livers

Ingredients:

1	container of frozen or fresh livers (chicken or beef)
1	cup flour in a brown paper bag
⅛	cup olive oil
3–4	portabella mushrooms, diced
1	medium to large yellow onion, diced

1. Dust livers with a light coating of flour in brown paper bag.
2. Cover bottom of skillet with olive oil and cook livers over medium to high heat until done to your liking.
3. Drain livers on paper towels to remove excess fat.
4. Cover livers with foil and place in a warm preheated oven at 150°F until ready to use.
5. Pour olive oil to cover bottom of large skillet. Add mushrooms and cook over medium-high heat for 10 minutes. Add chopped onions and continue cooking for another 10 minutes until moisture is reduced in mushrooms and onions are transparent.
6. Remove livers from oven and serve with mushrooms and onions on platter.

SERVES 4.

FROM LAND TO SEA

Linguini and Chicken
Strips in Peanut Sauce

Ingredients:

3	portabella mushrooms, diced
6	green onions, chopped
3	boned and skinned chicken breasts, strips
2	medium carrots, very thinly sliced
1	package of linguini
⅛	cup olive oil
	peanut sauce

1. Prepare onions and carrots. Do not cook.
2. Heat skillet with olive oil over medium-high heat and cook chicken strips for 15 minutes until golden brown.
3. Heat olive oil in a separate skillet over medium-high heat. Cook mushrooms until moisture is reduced, about 15 minutes.
4. In a separate soup pot, boil water and cook pasta per instructions and drain.
5. In a large bowl, toss drained pasta with cooked mushrooms, sautéed chicken and raw onions/carrots. Add enough peanut sauce to coat ingredients. Toss and serve immediately.

Serves 4–6.

FROM LAND TO SEA

Soft Shell Crab

Ingredients:

2	soft shell crabs, cleaned (you can purchase them cleaned)
2	cups flour
4	tbsp. Cajun seasoning
2	whole portabella mushrooms, remove stems
¼	cup olive oil

1. Put all flour and 3 tablespoons of Cajun seasoning in a bag. Place crabs in bag and shake till completely covered. Crabs should be lightly dusted with flour.
2. Brush both sides of mushrooms with olive oil. Sprinkle Cajun seasoning on both sides.
3. Prepare grill or broiler. Grill or broil mushrooms for 5–6 minutes on each side.
4. In large skillet, use remainder of olive oil to cover bottom of pan. Heat oil over medium-high heat. Cook crabs for 3 minutes on each side. Remove crabs from pan and place them on top of mushrooms. Set cap side up. Serve immediately.

SERVES 2.

*Option: Creamy Cajun sauce: ¼ cup whipping cream, 1 tsp. Cajun seasoning, 2 tbsp. flour, 1 tbsp. cream cheese, salt to taste. Create a sauce of your liking or use recommended creamy Cajun sauce. In saucepan, bring whipping cream to a boil. Add flour, Cajun seasoning and stir. Add small amount of cream cheese, stir and remove when thickened. Pour sauce over plate, stack crab on top of mushroom and serve.

Broiled Filet of Sole with Cream Sauce

Main Ingredients:

4	filets of sole
⅛	cup olive oil
	salt and pepper to taste

Ingredients for Portabella Cream Sauce:

1	portabella mushroom, diced
½	cup heavy cream
¼	cup onion, diced

1. Place seasoned filets evenly on broiling pan. Broil in preheated oven at 500°F or in gas range broiler, set on broil. Cook until browned, approximately 15 minutes.
2. Heat skillet, add oil to cover bottom of pan and add mushrooms. Cook over medium-high heat for 15 minutes. Add onions and sauté until transparent, about 5 minutes.
3. Blend mushrooms, onions and cream in a food processor until pureed. Put processor on setting #4.
4. Pour creamy puree in saucepan at low heat for 5–8 minutes.
5. When filets are done, remove immediately. Place each piece of fish on a plate and pour cream sauce over top. Serve immediately.

Serves 4.

FROM LAND TO SEA

Stuffed Trout with Portabella and Onions

Ingredients:

⅛	cup olive oil
2	portabella mushrooms, diced
1	medium onion, diced
4	fresh trout, cleaned, whole
	lemon pepper spice

1. In large skillet, at medium-high heat, cover bottom of pan with olive oil and sauté mushrooms for 10 minutes. When moisture is reduced, add onion and lemon pepper and cook for 5 minutes more. Remove from skillet.
2. Brush each trout lightly on outside with olive oil. Then, by spoonfuls, stuff whole cavity of each trout with mushroom/onion mixture.
3. Preheat oven to 375°F. Place trout on baking dish. Bake for 30–45 minutes until trout is crispy on outside. Serve immediately.

SERVES 4.

Seafood Fritter

Ingredients:

4	large prawns, shelled, diced
4	medium scallops, diced
6–8	green onions, diced
2	portabella mushrooms, diced
2	eggs, well beaten
1	clove garlic, minced
⅛	cup flour
⅛	cup corn meal
	spice (of your choice)
⅛	cup olive oil
	salt to taste

1. Place prawns, scallops, onions and mushrooms in a medium bowl with eggs and garlic. Mix thoroughly.
2. Add flour, corn meal, spice of your choice and salt. Mix all ingredients together. Mixture should be moist and adhere together to form a patty. If not, add a few drops of milk or water to moisten.
3. Form patties from the mixture and prepare to fry. Each patty should be 3" × 4" in size.
4. Heat skillet to medium high. Add oil to cover bottom of pan. Cook one seafood patty at a time, 4 minutes on each side. Cook until golden brown, for a total of 8–10 minutes. Do not crowd patties in the skillet as it will alter cooking time. When done, remove and place on paper towels to drain.
5. Continue cooking patties. Transfer cooked patties to a preheated 150ºF oven to keep warm. When ready to serve, remove from oven and plate. Serve immediately.

SERVES 4–6.

*Note: If more moisture is needed, add a few tablespoons of milk (or water).

Salmon, Spinach and Portabella Broil

Ingredients:

2	tbsp. oil (olive, corn, etc.)
2	tbsp. scallions, minced
2	(6 oz.) salmon filets or steaks
2	whole portabella mushrooms, stems removed
1	pound fresh spinach, wash carefully (or frozen)
3	tbsp. cream cheese
1	tbsp. crushed garlic
	salt and pepper to taste

1. Cut the filets or steaks into small bite-sized pieces.
2. Chop fresh spinach* and put in a microwaveable bowl with the cream cheese. Microwave long enough to melt the cream cheese, about 15–20 seconds. Or cook cream cheese in a saucepan over low heat. When cheese begins to melt, add fresh spinach. Cook for 5–8 minutes. Turn heat off. Mix in salt, pepper and crushed garlic. Chop the scallions and set aside.
3. Brush mushrooms (stems removed) with oil. Place them stemside up on a cookie sheet or baking dish. Broil for 3 minutes and remove. Raise oven to 375°F.
4. Place salmon pieces evenly on mushrooms (stemside up). Sprinkle with scallions, then spinach mixture, spreading it over each serving. Bake at 375°F for 20 minutes and serve hot (oven temperatures vary so check while cooking). All the ingredients will have melted and adhered to the mushrooms when done.

SERVES 2.

*Boil the frozen spinach for a few minutes until tender, drain well (squeeze out any excess moisture using a paper towel).

Stuffed Squid

Ingredients:

2	portabella mushrooms, sliced
1	medium onion, sliced
½	pound fresh squid, cleaned
¼	cup BBQ sauce (your favorite)
⅛	cup olive oil
	steamed rice

1. Heat the grill. Grill the portabellas and onions for 5–6 minutes on each side until done (vegetables should have no BBQ coating and no seasoning). When done, remove from grill, dice, then mix with BBQ sauce in a bowl.

2. Take cleaned fresh squid (squid should look shiny and firm with a gray color). If squid is pink or purple in coloration, this indicates that the squid is not fresh. Stuff squid with mushroom mixture, then 1–2 teaspoons of steamed rice. Make certain that rice and mushroom mixture is evenly spread inside of squid. Take toothpick and pierce each side of opening to squid to ensure closure while cooking.

3. Coat squid with olive oil and place on grill. Cook for 3–6 minutes, turning as cooking until browned. Do not overcook as squid will become tough. Serve immediately.

SERVES 6–8.

ITALIAN

Lasagna/Sun-Dried Tomato Sauce

Ingredients:

1	package lasagna noodles
3	portabella mushrooms, diced
1	medium sliced onion
⅛	cup olive oil
1	bunch spinach (leaves whole, washed, stems removed)
4	medium carrots, peeled, diced
1	cup mozzarella cheese, grated
2	cups sun-dried tomato sauce

1. In large soup pot, boil lasagna noodles per package instructions. When done, drain and have ready to use for assembly of lasagna ingredients.
2. Over medium-high heat, cover bottom of skillet with olive oil, add diced mushrooms and cook for 15 minutes. Add onions and cook for 7 minutes more or until transparent and starting to brown. Remove to a bowl.
3. Coat bottom of large 9" × 12" baking dish with your choice of sun-dried tomato sauce. Layer as follows: noodles, mushrooms/onions, whole leaves of spinach (enough to cover noodles), sliced carrots, grated cheese, then sauce. Repeat the process for four layers of noodles and filling, ending with noodles. Top the lasagna with cheese and sauce.
4. Cover with foil and bake at 400° F for 35–40 minutes. Remove from oven. Serve when done.

SERVES 6–8.

ITALIAN

Angel Hair Pasta and Peanut Sauce

Ingredients:

1	package angel hair pasta
3	portabella mushrooms, diced
⅛	cup olive oil
6	green onions, chopped
2	medium carrots, peeled, very thinly sliced
1	celery root, peeled, diced
	peanut sauce

1. Boil pasta per instructions and drain.
2. Heat skillet with olive oil over medium-high heat. Add mushrooms and cook for 15 minutes until moisture is reduced.
3. In a large bowl, toss drained pasta with cooked mushrooms and raw vegetables (onions, carrots, celery root). Add peanut sauce to taste. Toss and serve immediately.

SERVES 4–6.

Pesto Penne Pasta and Walnuts

Ingredients:

1	cup pesto sauce
1	tbsp. olive oil (for cooking pasta)
2	portabella mushrooms, diced
2	cups penne pasta
¼	cup finely chopped walnuts
⅛	cup olive oil (for cooking mushrooms)

1. In small saucepan cook pesto sauce over low heat for 5 minutes until it is heated.
2. Cover bottom of a large skillet with olive oil. Add mushrooms and cook over medium-high heat. Cook for 15 minutes until moisture is reduced.
3. In large soup pot boil water. Add salt and olive oil as needed. Add penne pasta and cook until done, as indicated on package. Remove and drain.
4. In large bowl toss pasta, mushrooms, pesto sauce and walnuts. Serve immediately.

Serves 6.

Stuffed Cannelloni and Béchamel Sauce

Ingredients:

	butter to grease baking dish
4	cannelloni shells (follow package instructions)
2	portabella mushrooms, diced
1	medium onion, diced
3	medium carrots, diced
1	medium red bell pepper, diced
⅓	cup parmesan cheese, grated
1	tbsp. olive oil (for cooking pasta)

Béchamel Sauce:

6	tsp. butter
¼	cup flour
2¼	cups milk
½	cup heavy whipping cream
2	egg yolks
⅔	cup parmesan cheese, grated
	salt and nutmeg to taste

1. Béchamel Sauce: At low heat melt butter in saucepan and whisk in flour all at once. Do not brown. Cook for 2–3 minutes. Stir in milk slowly with the whisk until it comes to a boil. Simmer for 10–15 minutes. Add cream while continuing to whisk. Remove from heat and let cool. Stir in one egg yolk at a time. Add cheese and seasoning. Whisk until smooth.

2. Preheat oven to 475°F. Butter a casserole dish.

3. Boil cannelloni according to box instructions. Remove when done.

4. At medium-high heat, add olive oil to cover bottom of large saute pan. Cook mushrooms for 15 minutes. Reduce heat; add onions, carrots and red bell pepper. Cook for 5–8 minutes.

5. Combine vegetables (step 4) and 2/3 of Béchamel sauce (step 1) in a large bowl and mix. Fill the shells with the mixture and place in baking dish. Cover with remaining sauce and grated cheese. Bake for 20 minutes.

SERVES 2–4.

Fettuccine Escargot and Portabellas

Ingredients:

⅛	cup olive oil
2	portabella mushrooms, diced
2	medium onions, diced
2	cloves garlic, minced
2	tsp. olive oil for pasta water
1	package of pasta (fettuccine)
14	oz. can escargot (snails), drained
	parmesan cheese
	salt (for pasta water)

1. Heat skillet, add olive oil to cover bottom of pan, add mushrooms and cook for 15 minutes at medium-high heat.
2. Add onions and sauté until transparent, about 10 minutes. Add garlic for 1–3 minutes. Do not overcook garlic (if it turns brown it will be bitter).
3. In large soup pot boil water. Add salt and olive oil to pot and cook fettuccine according to package instructions. Drain. Return to pot.
4. Remove mushrooms/onion/garlic mixture from skillet. If necessary add more olive oil and, in the same skillet, cook escargot over high heat for about 2 minutes, stirring constantly.
5. Add: mushrooms, onions, garlic and escargot to drained pasta. Toss and sprinkle with parmesan cheese. Serve immediately.

SERVES 6–8.

ITALIAN

Fresh Pasta Dough

Ingredients:

2⅓	cups unbleached flour
2	large eggs
4	egg yolks
½	tsp. salt
1	tbsp. olive oil
	warm water as needed

1. To mix dough by machine follow standard machine instructions. To mix dough by hand, it is preferred that your work surface be marble or wood. Pour flour into a mound with a hollow center or crater. Fill center with beaten eggs, egg yolks, salt and olive oil. Gradually work the flour into the egg center from the sides of the crater. Mix. When the dough starts to form a firm ball, lightly flour on the outside and start kneading with fingertips. If dough feels too moist, add a little flour while kneading. If dough becomes too dry add a little water as needed. After 8–10 minutes, dough should be elastic. Cover bowl with a damp cloth and let rest at room temperature for ½ hour to 2 hours before rolling.

2. Lightly dust work surface with flour. Cut dough into 3–4 pieces. Using rolling pin, roll each piece gently away from you toward the edge. Rotate and continue to roll until paper thin. Redust with flour lightly if needed. Use this recipe for any pasta dish such as raviolis, or even lasagna, etc., where you desire fresh homemade pasta rather than packaged pasta.

*3. **THIS STEP TO BE USED IN THE FOLLOWING TWO RECIPES:**

   Using a teaspoon, place mounds of filling 2 inches apart on top half of dough, leaving 1–1½ inches to edges. Before folding the bottom half of dough up moisten the edges of the dough with water and a pastry brush. Once moistened, then fold the bottom half of the dough to match the top half of the dough. Begin from center and work toward edges to remove air from pockets. Next, cut the dough into even squares between the pressed edges.

ITALIAN

Fried Cheese Ravioli Topped with Pesto and Mushroom

Ingredients for Filling:

1	cup goat cheese
1	cup parmesan cheese, grated
2	egg yolks
½	tsp. salt
	pepper to taste

1. Mix all of the ingredients in a small mixing bowl until goat cheese is crumbly. Entire mixture should be evenly coated with egg yolks and easy to mix with a large wooden spoon.
2. After making pasta dough use this filling to spoon small teaspoon mounds across the top half of the dough sheet 2 inches apart.
   Refer to *3 in **FRESH PASTA DOUGH** recipe.

Ingredients for Homemade Pesto:

(excellent pesto sauces can be found everywhere)

4	cloves minced garlic
⅓	cup pine nuts, ground
2½	cups fresh basil, washed, dried, chopped
1	cup parmesan cheese, grated
⅔	cup olive oil
	salt and pepper to taste

1. In blender: Mix minced garlic with pine nuts. Add basil to garlic and pine nuts. Add cheese to mixture. Continue to mix by adding olive oil and seasoning slowly until everything is blended.

Ingredients for Portabella Topping:

1	portabella mushroom, diced
½	diced onion
4	tbsp. olive oil

1. Heat skillet, add oil to cover bottom of pan and add mushrooms. Cook over medium-high heat for 15 minutes. Add onions and sauté until transparent, about 5 minutes.
2. Take separate large skillet, add ⅛ cup olive oil over medium-high heat. Fry raviolis, turning until golden brown. Remove when done and place on paper towels.
3. Turn heat down low and pour pesto over mushrooms and onions. Continue to cook for 2 minutes. Pour entire mixture over fried ravioli.

ITALIAN

Cajun Ravioli

Ingredients for Filling:

⅛	cup olive oil
2–3	portabellas, diced
2	tsp. Cajun seasoning
2	medium onions, diced

1. Coat bottom of large skillet with olive oil. Cook over medium-high heat and add diced mushrooms. Add Cajun seasoning and cook for 15 minutes until moisture is reduced from mushrooms. Add onions. Cook 5 minutes more.
2. Place mixture in a blender and reduce to a fine minced paste-like substance.
3. After making pasta dough use this filling to spoon small teaspoon mounds across the top half of the dough sheet 2 inches apart.
   Refer to *3 in **FRESH PASTA DOUGH** recipe.

Ingredients for Pasta Sauce:

½	cup whipping cream
2	tsp. Cajun seasoning

1. Pour cream in a saucepan and cook over medium heat until the cream comes to a rolling boil. Add Cajun seasoning and turn heat down to low. Cream should turn a slight orange/red color and thicken.

Instructions for Cooking Ravioli:

	water in soup pot
½	tsp. salt
1	tsp. olive oil
¼	cup parmesan cheese

1. In large soup pot, add salt and olive oil to water. Boil water to prepare for cooking ravioli. When boiling, add one ravioli at a time, stirring gently. Ten to twelve ravioli can be cooked at a time. Continue to cook. When ravioli rise to the top they should still be firm but tender, approximately 6–8 minutes.
2. Drain ravioli and place 6–8 in an individual serving bowl or plate. Top with creamy Cajun sauce. Sprinkle with parmesan cheese. Serve immediately.

SERVES 6–8.

ITALIAN

Portabella Parmigiano

Ingredients:

1	cup sun-dried tomato paste
1	cup garlic sun-dried tomato sauce
1	cup wine (red or white)
3	portabella mushrooms, sliced
3	raw eggs, beaten
1	cup bread crumbs
⅛	cup olive oil
1	bunch spinach (leaves whole, washed, stemmed)
1	cup mozzarella cheese, grated

1. In a large saucepan cook the tomato paste, garlic tomato sauce and wine over low heat for 2 hours until sauce thickens.
2. Preheat oven at 350°F for 30–45 minutes. Coat bottom of baking dish (9" × 12") with olive oil.
3. Dip portabella mushrooms in bowl of beaten eggs, then in bread crumbs. Repeat.
4. Place double-coated mushrooms in a baking dish. Cover with tomato mixture, whole spinach leaves and mozzarella. Bake in a preheated oven at 350°F for 30–45 minutes.

SERVES 4.

ITALIAN

Three-Tiered Portabella/Mozzarella

Ingredients:

3	whole portabella mushrooms, stems removed
6	cloves garlic, minced
⅛	cup olive oil
1	fresh rosemary sprig/branch (or 3 tsp. dried rosemary)
3	slices fresh mozzarella ⅛" thick

1. Grill or broil mushrooms until most of the moisture is gone from the mushrooms. Stir minced garlic in a saucepan with olive oil and rosemary. Heat for 5 minutes.
2. Put one mushroom cap side up, place one slice of fresh mozzarella on top. Pour garlic and rosemary mixture on top of mozzarella cheese. Repeat the process and arrange in three layers in an ovenproof dish and cook in preheated oven at 350ºF until the cheese melts. Cut into quarters to serve as appetizers.

Serves 4–6.

ITALIAN

Angel Hair in Cream Sauce

Ingredients:

2	portabella mushrooms, diced
⅛	cup olive oil
1	cup half and half
1	can white sauce (or make your own)
1	tsp. Creole seasoning
1	package angel hair pasta
6–8	green onions, chopped

1. In skillet over medium heat, cook mushrooms in olive oil for approximately 15 minutes until moisture is reduced.
2. In separate saucepan combine half and half, Creole seasoning and thickened white sauce (see below) or a can of white sauce. Stir over low heat for 15 minutes until well blended, then stir in mushrooms.
3. Cook angel hair pasta in large pot of boiling water. Drain pasta when done. Return to pot.
4. Toss cooked angel hair pasta with creamed mushroom mixture and add chopped green onions for color and flavor at the last minute. Toss and serve.

Serves 6.

Thickened White Sauce:

1	cup milk
¼	tsp. salt
⅛	tsp. black pepper
1	tbsp. corn starch (or white flour)
2	tsp. butter

1. Add ingredients to a saucepan at medium heat and let boil, approximately 1–2 minutes, stirring until thickened and creamy.

Pesto Lasagna

Ingredients:

1	package lasagna noodles
3	portabella mushrooms, diced
1	medium onion, sliced
⅛	cup olive oil
1	bunch spinach (leaves whole, washed, stems removed)
4	medium carrots, peeled, diced
1	cup mozzarella cheese, grated
3	cups pesto sauce

1. Boil noodles according to package instructions. When done, drain for assembly of lasagna.
2. Cover bottom of skillet with olive oil. Over medium-high heat, add diced mushrooms and cook for 15 minutes. Add onion and continue to cook for another 7 minutes or until onions are transparent and starting to brown. Remove mushroom/onion mixture to a bowl.
3. Coat bottom of large 9" × 12" glass baking dish with your choice of pesto sauce. Then begin the layering process as follows: boiled wide lasagna noodles, cooked mushroom/onions, whole leaves of spinach (enough to cover noodles), sliced carrots, grated cheese and sauce. Repeat the process, ending with lasagna noodles. Save enough cheese and sauce to top the lasagna with both. The end result will be four layers of noodles and filling.
4. Cover with foil and bake at 400ºF for 35–40 minutes. Serve when done.

SERVES 6–8.

ITALIAN

Sautéed Spinach over Polenta

Ingredients:

2–3	tbsp. unsalted butter
3–4	portabella mushrooms, diced
¼	cup chicken broth
¼	cup port wine
⅛	cup olive oil
1	bunch fresh spinach (whole, stems removed, wash even if prewashed)
1	tsp. nutmeg *Option: 1 tbsp. chives as garnish, or Cajun spice
1	12-oz. package of polenta (local grocery)
1	4-oz. package of fresh mozzarella cheese
	salt and pepper to taste

1. In large skillet melt butter over medium-high heat. Add mushrooms and cook for 15 minutes. Remove mushrooms. In same skillet add chicken broth and port wine. Cook at high heat until liquid is reduced by half. Return mushrooms to skillet in reduced broth and keep warm.

2. In another skillet at medium-high heat lightly cover bottom with olive oil. Add washed spinach leaves and cook briefly until wilted. Add nutmeg, salt and pepper to taste. Remove from skillet. Use this skillet for step 3.

3. Follow preparation instructions on polenta package. Try cutting in ¼-inch slices. At medium-high heat cover bottom of skillet with olive oil and cook polenta slices, turning over once. Top with a slice of fresh mozzarella. Continue cooking until cheese melts, approximately 4 minutes.

4. On a serving plate, place a slice of polenta on bed of spinach and top with several spoonfuls of mushroom mixture. Garnish with chopped chives or Cajun spice. Serve immediately.

Serves 4–6.

Cannelloni Stuffed with Mushrooms

Ingredients:

½	medium onion, diced
½	bunch spinach, washed, with stems removed
½	cup parmesan cheese, grated
2	portabella mushrooms, diced
15	fresh basil leaves, chopped
3	cloves minced garlic
1	package cannelloni shells (follow package instructions)
⅛	cup olive oil
	red tomato sauce of your choice

1. In a medium bowl, place washed, stemmed spinach leaves. Be sure to hand wash each leaf of spinach (even if you buy prewashed spinach leaves, they are not always completely dirt free!).
2. Cover bottom of large skillet with olive oil. Add portabella mushrooms and cook over medium-high heat for 15 minutes until moisture is reduced. Add onions and minced garlic and continue cooking for 5 minutes more or until onions are transparent. Remove immediately. Do not let garlic brown!
3. In large soup pot bring water to boil, add salt and when boiling, add cannelloni shells. Cook according to package instructions. Remove when done and drain.
4. Stuffing: In one large bowl mix: cheese, mushrooms, onions, garlic, spinach and fresh basil leaves.
5. Stuff each boiled cannelloni shell with the stuffing mixture.
6. Pour your favorite red tomato sauce over the top.
7. Bake in preheated oven at 400° F for 20 minutes or until bubbly and done.

Serves 6–8.

Pasta with Portabellas

Ingredients:

⅓	cup olive oil
3	portabella mushrooms, diced
½	cup whipping cream (not whipped)
4–6	tbsp. Cajun seasoning
1	package pasta (vermicelli preferred)

1. Heat olive oil in skillet; cook mushrooms for 15 minutes. Add Cajun seasoning. Cook for 5 minutes more. Set aside.
2. Cook cream in saucepan over medium heat until the cream comes to a rolling boil and thickens. Turn heat off. Add to skillet with mushrooms. Toss to coat mushrooms completely with cream and spices. Cream should turn a slight orange/red due to spices.
3. Boil pasta per package instructions in a large soup pot, drain and add creamy mushroom mixture to pasta. Serve immediately.

SERVES 4–6.

Pizza Portabella Style

Topping Ingredients:

	red sauce of your choice (if desired)
1	cup mozzarella cheese, grated
1	medium sweet onion, thinly sliced
1	portabella mushroom, sliced very thinly

Ingredients for Pizza Dough:

1¼	cups warm water
1	tsp. active dry yeast
2	tbsp. olive oil
3½	cups flour
1½	tsp. salt

1. In a large bowl, combine water, yeast and oil. Stir continuously with a large wooden spoon, add flour and salt until the dough forms a moist firm ball.
2. Place dough on a floured work surface. Knead until smooth and elastic, approximately 5 minutes.
3. Place kneaded dough in a large lightly oiled bowl. Cover with a damp cloth. Let dough rise until swollen and nearly double in bulk (approximately 1 hour).
4. Cut risen dough in half, and place each piece in a separate oiled bowl. Cover with damp cotton cloth and let rise for approximately 20 minutes.
5. Grease rounded pizza pan. Take one half of risen dough and round and flatten outward from center, rotating the pan as you go. Diameter should be about 12 inches. Repeat process with second half of risen dough.
6. Top with sauce, cheese, onion and mushrooms (in that order). Bake in preheated oven at 425°F for 15 minutes, or until bubbly and golden brown at the edges. Serve immediately.

Parmesan Crusted with Rosemary Vegetables

Ingredients:

4	zucchini, sliced
12	asparagus (well washed)
1	orange bell pepper, sliced
1	red bell pepper, sliced
1	sprig of rosemary
	Italian Dressing recipe (see page xii)
2	eggs, beaten
1	cup parmesan cheese, grated
1	cup bread crumbs
4	portabella mushrooms, sliced
⅛	cup olive oil

1. In a bowl, marinate mixed sliced vegetables (bell pepper, asparagus, zucchini) in Italian seasoning mixture with sprig of rosemary for approximately 30–40 minutes.
2. BBQ or broil vegetables for 5–6 minutes, until charbroiled. Remove immediately to a platter.
3. In a bowl, mix bread crumbs and parmesan cheese. Beat eggs in a shallow dish. Dip mushrooms in egg and then bread crumb mixture.
4. Cover bottom of large skillet with olive oil and heat over medium-high heat. Place each breaded slice of mushroom in hot skillet and fry until golden brown on all sides (turn every 2 minutes). Remove to a paper towel to absorb excess oil.
5. Arrange grilled vegetables and mushrooms on a platter and serve immediately.

SERVES 6–8.

ASIAN

Steamed Rice

Ingredients:

⅛	cup olive oil
4	portabella mushrooms, diced
2	medium onions, diced
2	cups cooked white rice

1. Add olive oil to skillet and cook diced mushrooms for 10 minutes over medium-high heat until moisture is reduced. Add onions to mushrooms and cook for another 5 minutes until onions are transparent and brown.
2. Fill small serving bowls with rice, and top with mushroom/onion mixture.

Serves 6.

Fried Rice

Ingredients:

⅛	cup olive oil
4	portabella mushrooms, diced
2	medium onions, diced
2	medium carrots, diced
2	medium stalks of celery, diced
¼	pound of peas (canned/frozen)
2	eggs, beaten
2	cups cooked white rice
3	tbsp. soy sauce to taste

1. Add olive oil to skillet and cook diced mushrooms for 10 minutes over medium-high heat until moisture is reduced. Add onions to mushrooms and cook for 5 minutes until onions are transparent and brown.
2. Add carrots, celery, peas and eggs to skillet. Cook for 5 minutes until vegetables are mixed well and eggs are cooked.
3. Add cooked white steamed rice to skillet. Stir over medium heat for 5–10 minutes until carrots are tender. Add soy sauce (or sauce of your choice) when stirring. Serve immediately.

SERVES 6.

Spring Roll

Ingredients:

⅛	cup peanut oil or sesame seed oil
2	portabella mushrooms, diced
6–8	green onions, chopped
2	medium carrots, diced
½	pound bean sprouts, washed
1	package won ton skins (Option: rice paper)
1	egg yolk (or water to moisten edges of won ton)
	plum sauce (found in local grocery Asian section)

1. Heat skillet, add oil to cover bottom of pan and add mushrooms. Cook over medium-high heat for 10 minutes. Add onions and sauté with mushrooms for another 5 minutes until transparent.

2. In small pot boil water and add diced carrots. Cook carrots for 2–3 minutes, just enough to parboil and soften before adding to spring roll. Remove carrots from water immediately.

3. In a separate bowl mix together: mushrooms, onions, carrots and uncooked bean sprouts. Prepare won ton skins one at a time in a spacious work area. Moisten edges of each won ton skin with water or egg yolk.

4. Place 1–2 tablespoons of filling in the center of the won ton skin. Starting with the edge closest to you, begin rolling away from you until completely sealed. Place on a plate with the seam side down.

5. In a separate skillet heat oil over high heat. When skillet is ready, fry spring rolls a few at a time (4–6) seam side down. Do not crowd spring rolls in the skillet as it will alter cooking time. Turn and cook each spring roll until golden brown. Remove and place on paper towels to drain. Serve plum sauce in a small decorative bowl as a dipping sauce. Serve immediately.

Serves 4–6.

Stir Fried with Veggies

Ingredients:

⅛	cup sesame seed oil
2	portabella mushrooms, diced
1	medium onion, diced
1	medium carrot, peeled, sliced
1	medium celery stalk, diced
1	yellow bell pepper, diced
1	green bell pepper, diced
1	zucchini, diced
½	cup bean sprouts
1–2	tsp. soy sauce
	*Optional: wok

1. Add oil to cover bottom of large skillet (or wok). Heat over medium-high heat. Add mushrooms and cook for 10 minutes.
2. Add the following to mushroom skillet: onions, carrot, celery, bell peppers, zucchini, bean sprouts. Sauté until done (approximately 5 minutes).
3. Just prior to removing from skillet, add soy sauce and toss vegetables until evenly coated. Serve immediately over white rice.

Serves 4–6.

154

Stir Fried on Wilted Spinach

Ingredients:

⅛	cup olive oil
3	portabella mushrooms, diced
3	large onions, diced
2	bunches of fresh spinach (washed and stems removed)
2	tbsp. olive oil (to cook spinach)

1. Heat skillet, add olive oil to cover bottom of pan and add mushrooms. Cook over medium heat for 10 minutes.
2. Add onions to mushrooms and continue to cook until transparent (approximately 5 minutes).
3. Preheat a separate skillet over medium-high heat. Add olive oil. Cook fresh spinach until it wilts. Serve each plate with spinach on bottom, topped with mushroom/onion mixture. Can be served over rice if preferred.

SERVES 4.

Bok Choy and Black Bean Sauce

Ingredients:

⅛	cup sesame seed oil
1	portabella mushroom, diced
1	tbsp. black bean sauce
½	tbsp. soy sauce
2–3	tbsp. chicken broth
¼	tsp. sugar
1	bunch bok choy (washed and separated)

1. Heat skillet or wok over medium-high heat. Add oil to cover bottom of pan, and add mushrooms. Cook for 15 minutes. Remove.
2. In the same skillet add the black bean sauce, soy sauce, chicken broth and sugar. Cook for 1 minute.
3. Return mushrooms to the wok or skillet and continue cooking for another 5 minutes. Add bok choy and cook for 2 minutes, or until dark green. Serve immediately.

SERVES 4.

ASIAN

Chow Mein

Ingredients:

3	tbsp. soy sauce
1	tsp. brown sugar
1	tsp. sweet chili sauce
1	small piece ginger root, finely chopped
3	portabella mushrooms, diced
½	pound egg noodles (available in local grocery or Asian store)
1	tsp. cornstarch
6	tbsp. chicken stock (*Option: vegetable broth)
3	tbsp. corn oil
4	green onions, chopped
1	medium celery stalk, diced
1	medium carrot, diced
2	cups bean sprouts

1. In a large bowl mix: soy sauce, brown sugar and chili sauce. Marinate mushrooms for 30 minutes, stirring every 10 minutes. Remove from marinade liquid. Mix marinade with cornstarch and chicken stock. Set aside.
2. Cook noodles according to package instructions. Drain and set aside.
3. In a wok or large skillet, heat corn oil over medium-high heat. Add: ginger root and mushrooms. Cook for 10 minutes. Add: onions, celery, carrot, bean sprouts and noodles. Stir and cook for 5 minutes. Add marinade mixture and stir-fry until sauce thickens and vegetables are evenly coated. Serve immediately.

SERVES 4–6.

Sesame Ginger BBQ Chicken

Ingredients:

2	tsp. sesame seeds, toasted
4	tbsp. honey
4	tbsp. soy sauce
4	tsp. ginger root, peeled, grated
4	chicken breasts, boned, skinned, halved
4	portabella mushrooms (sliced one-inch thick)
6	green onions, diced (use as garnish)

1. Marinade: In a bowl mix: sesame seeds, honey, soy sauce and ginger root. Marinate sliced mushrooms for 15–20 minutes prior to grilling, stirring mushrooms every 5 minutes to ensure even coating. Remove mushrooms from bowl and place on plate. Reserve marinade for basting chicken breasts when grilling.

2. Place chicken on cutting board between two sheets of plastic wrap. Flatten chicken breasts.

3. Prepare BBQ grill. Coals are ready when white and hot. Place chicken breasts on grill. Cook for 8–12 minutes, turning every 5 minutes until golden brown. Baste chicken frequently after it has cooked for a minimum of 5 minutes on each side. BASTING WILL BURN RAW CHICKEN! Remove when done.

4. Place sliced mushrooms on the BBQ grill and cook for 15 minutes until moisture is reduced. Remove when done.

5. Each serving includes one grilled breast and a few sliced portabella mushrooms with diced green onions sprinkled on top. Serve immediately.

SERVES 4.

Malaysian Curry Style

Ingredients:

⅛	cup sesame seed oil
1	clove garlic
½	medium onion, diced
3	portabella mushrooms, diced
½	tsp. medium-hot curry powder (Malaysian if possible)
2	tsp. oyster sauce
4	tbsp. coconut milk
¼	red bell pepper, diced
¼	yellow bell pepper, diced
2	red chili peppers, diced
½	tomato, diced
¼	cup water
	sugar to taste

1. Add oil to cover bottom of wok or large skillet. Over medium-high heat add the following: garlic, onion, mushrooms. Cook for 7 minutes.

2. In the same skillet, add curry powder, stir and cook for ½ minute (do not burn). Continue stirring and add oyster sauce and coconut milk. Cook for 1–2 minutes.

3. Add remaining ingredients: bell pepper, chili peppers, sugar, water and tomato. Continue to cook for 2–3 minutes or until peppers are tender and liquid thickens. Serve immediately over steamed rice.

SERVES 6.

MEXICAN & CAJUN

Portabella Burrito

Ingredients:

6–8	portabella mushrooms, diced
⅛	cup olive oil
4	large flour tortillas
2	medium tomatoes, chopped
1	cup shredded iceberg lettuce (or cabbage)
1	cup cheddar cheese, grated
	salsa to taste
	Mexican seasoning to taste

1. Pour olive oil to cover bottom of large skillet. Add mushrooms and cook over medium heat for 20 minutes till moisture is reduced. Add seasoning.
2. Put seasoned mushroom mixture into center of warmed tortillas. Add: tomatoes, lettuce, cheese and salsa as garnish. Fold the tortilla end closest to you toward the opposite end over the filling. Then, fold two sides of the tortilla toward the center and roll burrito away from you. Burrito is ready to eat. Continue to fill all four tortillas.

SERVES 4.

Portabella Tacos

Ingredients:

6–8	portabella mushrooms, diced
⅛	cup olive oil
2	medium tomatoes, chopped
1	cup shredded iceberg lettuce (or cabbage)
1	cup cheddar cheese, grated
	salsa to taste
	Mexican seasoning to taste
	corn tortillas or taco shells

1. Pour olive oil to cover bottom of large skillet. Add mushrooms and cook over medium heat for 20 minutes until moisture is reduced. Add seasoning.
2. Put mushroom mixture into center of warmed tortillas or taco shells; add: tomatoes, lettuce, cheese and salsa as garnish.

SERVES 3–4.

Quesadillas

Ingredients:

⅛	cup olive oil
2	portabella mushrooms, diced
1	medium onion, diced
4	large flour tortillas
½	cup mild cheddar cheese, grated
½	cup Mexican cheese, grated

1. Over medium-high heat, cover bottom of a skillet with olive oil. Add mushrooms to skillet. Cook for 10 minutes and then add sliced onions and continue to cook for 5 minutes until onion is transparent. When done, remove from skillet immediately and place mixture in a bowl.

2. Take large flour tortilla and place on flat oiled pan. With tortilla open, sprinkle both grated cheeses and mushroom mixture into middle of cooking tortilla on pan. Let cook for 1–3 minutes until cheese begins to melt. Fold tortilla in half and continue to cook for 3 minutes or until cheese is visibly melted in tortilla. Continue to cook each tortilla until all four are done. Serve immediately.

Serves 2–4.

MEXICAN & CAJUN

Tostada

Ingredients:

⅛	cup olive oil
1	can pinto beans
2	portabella mushrooms, diced
1	tomato, diced
1	cup mild cheddar cheese, grated
6–9	green onions, chopped
½	head iceberg lettuce (or cabbage), shredded
	one package tostada shells

1. Take skillet and cover bottom with olive oil. Sauté diced mushrooms over medium-high heat for 10–15 minutes until moisture is reduced. Remove from skillet and place in bowl when done.
2. Take small saucepan and heat pinto beans. Remove.
3. Prepare bowls of ingredients listed above: tomatoes, cheese, onions and lettuce.
4. Take tostada and layer with cooked mushrooms, pinto beans and remainder of ingredients (step 3). Serve immediately.

SERVES 4–6.

Portabella Nachos

Ingredients:

⅛	cup olive oil
1	cup mild cheddar cheese, grated
1	bag tortilla chips
2	portabella mushrooms, diced
1–2	cups cooked whole black beans*
1	tomato, diced
6–9	green onions, chopped
¼	cup sliced fresh jalapeños

1. Heat skillet. Add olive oil to cover bottom of pan, and add mushrooms. Cook over medium-high heat for 10–15 minutes. Remove immediately.
2. In a separate saucepan, heat black beans.
3. Take 2–3 cups of chips and place on plate, pan or platter which can be heated in the oven. Sprinkle with grated cheese. Place in preheated oven at 425°F for 5 minutes or until cheese is melted and chips are warmed. Remove from oven.
4. Place chips and melted cheese on individual plates. Add mushrooms. Pour ¼ cup of black beans over mushrooms. Top the nachos with the remainder of the uncooked ingredients: tomatoes, onions and jalapeños. Serve immediately.

SERVES 2–3.

*Or, if you choose, one can of black beans, or one can of refried beans.

MEXICAN & CAJUN

Creole/Cajun Portabella Sandwich

Ingredients:

4	portabella mushrooms, sliced
2	medium onions, sliced
2	tsp. Creole seasoning (or more to taste)
2	medium tomatoes, sliced
¼	head iceberg lettuce, shredded (or lettuce of your choice)
4	soft French bread buns, split
⅛	cup olive oil

1. Cover bottom of pan with ⅛ cup olive oil. Heat skillet to medium heat. Add sliced mushrooms and cook for 10 minutes. Add onions and creole seasoning; sauté onions for 5 minutes, until transparent.
2. Heat French buns in preheated oven at 350°F until warm, about 5–8 minutes.
3. Place mushrooms and onions generously on bottom of heated bun, add sliced tomatoes and lettuce and cover with top of bun. Serve immediately.

SERVES 4.

Spicy Mediterranean Tomato Sauce

Ingredients:

⅛	cup olive oil
2	portabella mushrooms, sliced
¼	cup plain yogurt
¼	tsp. paprika
2	tsp. mild curry powder
¼	cup tomato paste

1. At medium-high heat cover bottom of skillet with olive oil. Add sliced mushrooms and cook for 10–15 minutes until moisture is removed. Remove from heat.
2. In a separate skillet over low heat mix: yogurt, paprika, curry powder and tomato paste. Warm until well blended and creamy.
3. Add cooked mushrooms. Mix together until all mushroom slices are evenly coated with sauce. Serve immediately.

SERVES 4.

MEXICAN & CAJUN

Enchiladas

Ingredients:

2	portabella mushrooms, diced
⅛	cup olive oil
2	medium onions, diced
1	can black olives, whole, pitted
1	cup Mexican cheese, grated
1	cup mild cheddar cheese, grated
2	cups enchilada sauce
	steamed rice
	12 corn tortillas

1. Cook diced mushrooms in pan with olive oil over medium-high heat for approximately 10 minutes until moisture from mushrooms is reduced. Add onions to same skillet and continue cooking for 5 more minutes or until onions are transparent and browning. Remove from heat. Pour mushroom/onion mixture into bowl.

2. Take 9" × 12" glass baking dish and set aside. Get organized by preparing and putting each ingredient in its own bowl (olives, cheese, portabellas, onions, rice, etc.). Now you have your own assembly line set up for making the enchiladas.

3. Cover bottom of skillet with olive oil, and heat each tortilla over low-medium heat until soft and pliable – not too firm. (This skillet is to be used for tortillas only.)

4. Pour the enchilada sauce into a wide pan and cook over low-medium heat (to dredge the tortilla in sauce – see below).

5. In this series of steps you will be doing the following:
   A. Cook each tortilla in a skillet of oil for 1–2 minutes (step 3).
   B. Remove the cooked tortilla from the oil and dredge it through heated enchilada sauce just to moisten it (step 4).
   C. Fill the tortilla with mushrooms/onions, two cheeses, steamed rice and olives.
   D. Roll tortilla closed.

6. Continue cooking and filling and rolling each tortilla until the glass baking dish has 8–12 rolled tortillas. Place extra olives on the sides. Pour enchilada sauce over filled and rolled tortillas. Sprinkle top of enchiladas with remaining cheese. Cover with foil and bake in a 350°F preheated oven for 30 minutes. Serve immediately.

SERVES 6–8.

MEXICAN & CAJUN

Cajun Potato Wedges

Ingredients:

3	medium potatoes, washed, cut into wedges
⅛	cup olive oil
2	portabella mushrooms, sliced
3	cloves garlic, minced
1	medium red onion
1–2	tsp. Cajun powder
1	tsp. salt

1. Wash and cut potatoes into wedges (skin on). Bake wedges at 350°F for 40 minutes until golden brown.
2. Cover bottom of large skillet with olive oil. Add mushrooms and cook over medium-high heat. Cook for 10 minutes until moisture is reduced. Add: minced garlic, red onion and Cajun powder. Cook for 5 minutes more.
3. Arrange potatoes and top with mushroom mixture. Serve immediately.

SERVES 4–6.

Cajun Mushroom Puffed Pastry

Ingredients:

3	medium potatoes, washed, peeled, diced
⅛	cup olive oil
2	portabella mushrooms, diced
3	cloves garlic, minced
1	medium onion, diced
1	carrot, peeled, sliced
1–2	tsp. Cajun powder

1. Cover potatoes with water in large soup pot and boil for 15 minutes or until done. Remove and dice.
2. In large skillet add ⅛ cup olive oil (enough to cover bottom of pan). Add mushrooms and cook over medium heat for 10 minutes until moisture is reduced. Add minced garlic, potatoes, onion, carrot and Cajun powder, and continue to cook for 5 minutes more. Remove from heat.

Ingredients for Pastry Dough:

1	package frozen puff pastry dough
1	egg beaten

1. Roll out thawed pastry dough and cut into ¼" × 6" square pieces. Make eight squares.
2. Fill center of square with 2–4 teaspoons of mushroom filling (see above). Then, fold over diagonally into a triangle. Brush pastry edges with egg and crimp edges to seal. Glaze with beaten egg.
3. Place triangles on baking sheet. Bake in preheated oven at 400°F. Bake for 15–20 minutes or until golden brown. Serve immediately.

SERVES 4.

Grilled with Fried Yucca

Ingredients:

1	package of frozen yucca (from local Latin grocery)
6	portabella mushrooms, sliced
¼	cup olive oil (to be used for mushrooms)
¼	cup chili powder
2	medium cucumbers, peeled, sliced
8	green onions, chopped
2	medium tomatoes, sliced
	salt to taste
	olive oil (to fry yucca)

1. In a large soup pot, boil yucca according to instructions (approximately 30–45 minutes). Remove and drain.
2. In a large bowl coat sliced mushrooms with olive oil and chili powder.
3. Prepare BBQ* grill until coals are white and hot. Cook mushrooms for 15 minutes until moisture is reduced. Turn every 5 minutes. Remove when done.
4. In a large skillet pour 1–2 inches of olive oil. Heat to medium-high for 6 minutes, then fry yucca until golden brown. Remove and drain on paper towels.
5. Place grilled portabella mushrooms on platter with the fried yucca. Garnish by placing sliced cucumbers and tomatoes around edge of platter. Top with chopped green onions. Serve immediately.

SERVES 4–6.

*Although this recipe calls for grilling outside on a BBQ grill, you could use an indoor grill. An alternative would be to saute the mushrooms in ⅛ cup olive oil over medium-high heat for 10–15 minutes.

Note: I prefer grilling the mushrooms outdoors to avoid cooking both main ingredients in oil.

Recipe Index